HIDDEN STORIES
IN PLANTS

HIDDEN STORIES
IN PLANTS

Unusual and Easy-to-Tell Stories
from Around the World
Together with Creative Things
to Do While Telling Them

Anne Pellowski

Illustrated by Lynn Sweat

Macmillan Publishing Company
New York

Collier Macmillan Publishers
London

By the same author

THE STORY VINE
A Source Book of Unusual and Easy-to-Tell Stories
from Around the World

THE FAMILY STORYTELLING HANDBOOK
How to Use Stories, Anecdotes, Rhymes, Handkerchiefs, Paper,
and Other Objects to Enrich Your Family Traditions

Text copyright © 1990 by Anne Pellowski
Illustrations copyright © 1990 by Lynn Sweat
All rights reserved. No part of this book may be reproduced or
transmitted in any form or by any means, electronic or mechanical,
including photocopying, recording, or by any information storage
and retrieval system, without permission in writing from the Publisher.
Macmillan Publishing Company
866 Third Avenue, New York, NY 10022
Collier Macmillan Canada, Inc.
First Edition
Printed in the United States of America

10   9   8   7   6   5   4   3   2   1

The text of this book is set in 12 point Times Roman.
The illustrations are rendered in pen-and-ink.

Library of Congress Cataloging-in-Publication Data
Pellowski, Anne.
Hidden stories in plants: unusual and easy-to-tell stories
from around the world, together with creative things to do
while telling them / by Anne Pellowski. — 1st ed.   p.   cm.
Includes bibliographical references.
Summary: Presents myths, legends, tales, and folklore about
plants and describes how to use plants to make ornaments,
toys, disguises, dolls, and musical instruments.
ISBN 0-02-770611-7
1. Plants—Folklore.   2. Tales.   [1. Plants—Folklore.
2. Folklore.   3. Nature craft.   4. Handicraft.]   I. Title.
PZ8.1.P37Hi   1990   398.24′2—dc20   89-37166   CIP   AC

Dedicated to
Ellen, Heidi, Stephanie,
April, Marissa, and Jennifer

Contents

Acknowledgments

Thanks to the following for their creative ideas in making ornaments, play-things, disguises, dolls, and musical instruments: Angie, Betsy, Bette, Chad, Dan, Denny, Dick, Donna, Dorothy, Emily, Eric, Gary, Gerry, Heather, Holly, Janie, Jeff, Karianne, Kathy B., Kathy L., Keith, Kevin, Kyla, Larry, Laurie, Linda, Millie, Nicole, Robbie, Roman, Sara, Shadow, Steve, and Steven Peter. Most of the activities pictured here are based on actual photos taken at Willow Wind Farm in Wisconsin and in Williamstown, Mass.

Thanks also to Asenath Odaga, Susan Patron, Mabel Ross, and Somboon Singkamanen.

I am also grateful for special assistance at the following libraries: Central Children's Room, New York Public Library; Columbia University Library; Library of Congress, General Reference Division; Houghton Library, Harvard University.

Introduction

This book is for people who enjoy sharing walks through parks, woods, and along streams, or just sitting together in gardens, kitchens, or classrooms, admiring the special qualities of plants. It is especially for those who like to fantasize about the unusual shapes of the natural things they see. It is also for those who like to tell or listen to short stories about flowers, trees, and other plants in the natural environment.

The stories and activities suggested here are meant to be as spontaneous as possible. Only natural objects found in woods, fields, parks, gardens, or kitchens are used. The single recommended tool is a small pocket knife, and even that is not always necessary.

The basic idea is to notice the beauty and diversity of plant life, by telling stories about plants and by using the parts of plants nature (or a human) discards to make amusing creations. These creations are meant to be ephemeral and enjoyed partly for that quality.

The stories are myths, legends, tales, and folklore from different peoples and places throughout the world. Most of them are short and can be told in less than five minutes. They are related in simple, easy-to-tell versions that should not prove too difficult for even the novice storyteller.

I recommend telling them in the quiet moments before, during, or after a nature walk; in a kitchen while preparing food; or during a seasonal story hour in a classroom or library. Above all, I advocate using spare language that is without the weight of heavy explanations or moralizing.

Like the floss of dandelions and milkweed, these stories should continue to be sent floating out into the wide world, in much the same way they have drifted down to us across the centuries. By telling them, we keep alive our wonder at the tremendous variety of life on our planet.

Before You Begin

Picking hundreds of dandelions will hardly change the supply of that ubiquitous plant. However, many wildflowers, ferns, and other plants are not as plentiful as dandelions. Some are disappearing so quickly that they have been placed on lists of endangered species.

Be aware of those flowers and plants that are becoming scarce or even rare. Find out from your local Parks Department, or the State Department of Natural Resources in your area, about plants that are protected and those that are becoming so scarce they soon will have to be on the endangered list.

Most of the activities in this book are meant to be carried out with garden flowers, or with parts of plants that are being discarded, such as carrot tops. Seeds, leaves, petals, blossoms, bark, and branches that have blown off in the wind are plentiful in many areas. Use such materials first, and resort to picking parts of fresh plants only when they are very numerous, or, as in some cases, a nuisance. Pluck off a few buds or stems from clumps that are very thick. Spread your picking efforts over as wide an area as possible.

Be sure all participants know if they are allergic to plants, and know how to recognize such irritating plants as poison ivy, poison oak, poison sumac, and others, if they are common to the area you choose for your nature walks and stories. Caution participants never to put any parts of plants into their mouths.

HIDDEN STORIES
IN PLANTS

PART ONE

Ornaments

When walking through a field or forest filled with blooming plants, many people have a desire to pluck one of the flowers and put it behind an ear or tuck it in the hair. This inclination to make body ornaments out of natural things has been around for a long time.

Since ancient times, people have been using flowers or leaves to make wreaths for the head or garlands for the neck. Olympic athletes were honored in this way. Rulers had crowns of leaves long before they wore jeweled or golden crowns. Religious rites in honor of certain gods or goddesses were performed by people wearing wreaths or garlands.

Some of these old customs have survived. Schools or groups in certain communities still crown a May queen with flowers. People in many parts of the Pacific islands continue to give flower necklaces as a special sign of welcome.

On a walk through country fields, gardens, and meadows, watch out for plants such as: daisies, dandelions, clover, knotweed, pinks, fleabane, primroses, violets, pansies, buttercups, gentian, wild bergamot or beebalm, day lilies, coneflowers, and pickerelweed.

While preparing carrots or other vegetables in the kitchen, rather than discarding the leafy tops, make a crown or necklace by braiding them.

Tell the following stories while you carry out your activities or at any time they strike you as appropriate.

Stories to Tell

THE WREATHS OF WISDOM
Greek and Roman Legend

In ancient times, leaves on trees and plants were believed to know all secrets.

One day, a magician decided to make a wreath of leaves. He put it on his head so that it rested just above his ears. He hoped to listen closely to all the secret things the leaves might whisper to each other.

The magician grew wise and powerful. Other magicians copied his idea and made themselves wreaths of leaves. Gradually, it became the custom to crown a person with a wreath of leaves, to show that the person was recognized as having great wisdom.

THE DAISY
English Folklore

The sun is the day's eye, because it looks down on us like a giant eye from above, but only during the daytime hours.

When people first saw the flower we call a daisy, some began to call it the "day's eye" because the bright yellow center, surrounded by white petals, reminded them of the sun above, with its white-hot rays in summer. Soon, it was easier to say "daisy" rather than "day's eye" and that is what the flower has been called ever since.

French-speaking peoples call the flower *marguerite* and in Spanish it is likewise named *margarita*. One of the legends that explains this name tells of Sainte Marguerite who, in her prayers, always turned her face up to heaven.

RANUNCULUS
Roman Myth

The Latin name for buttercup is *Ranunculus,* which means "little frog." Some say this is so because buttercups like to grow in the same cool, wet places where frogs like to live. Others say that the flower has this name because of the sound the frogs make when they call out.

A long time ago, so the story goe: a bright and merry boy named Ranunculus came each morning to sing and dance. He always wore a robe of shining yellow satin. But one day he did not appear and the frogs looked for him in vain. They continue to call out, asking him to come: "Ranunculus! Ranunculus!" And Ranunculus, the buttercup, comes back each spring so as not to disappoint the frogs.

SHAWONDASEE AND THE GOLDEN GIRL
Ojibwa Tale

In the summer, Shawondasee, the south wind, grew heavy, drowsy, lazy. He liked to lie in the shade of live oaks and magnolias, inhaling deeply the odor of the blossoms and filling his lungs so full that when he exhaled, his breath carried with it a delicate perfume.

One day Shawondasee gazed over his fields with a sleepy eye and saw at a distance a slender girl with yellow hair. He admired her and wanted to call her to his side, but he felt too lazy.

Next morning he looked again, and she was still there, more beautiful than ever. Every day he looked, and held his breath for a few moments, until he saw the girl in the warm green prairie grass.

One morning, as Shawondasee awoke and glanced over the fields, he rubbed his eyes.

His golden girl was gone! Instead, an old woman stood there, with head of gray.

"My brother, the north wind, has been here and put his cruel hand on her head!" cried Shawondasee.

He gave such a mighty sigh that the old woman's hair fell from her head and she was gone.

WHY THERE ARE VIOLETS IN MEADOWS
Greek Myth

Zeus, king of the gods, passed by a meadow one day and there he saw a lovely girl, Io. He fell in love with her instantly. He wanted only to spend his idle hours with Io, lazing about in the grass.

But Hera, the wife of Zeus, became jealous. She did not like to see him admiring Io so much.

Then Zeus used his great power and changed Io into a young heifer, hoping that Hera would not notice her. But when Zeus saw Io grazing on the grass of the field, he decided that it was too coarse and common a food for one so lovely.

So he caused a new flower to grow and cover the field. It was delicate in size and subtle in scent, and its color was a royal purple, indicating it was fit for the gods.

And ever since then those flowers, the violets, can be found in meadows.

WHY THE PANSY HAS NO FRAGRANCE
German Legend

Long, long ago, so long ago that I have forgotten why, a grateful nymph wished to reward a poor farmer and his wife. The couple owned only a small cottage and a bit of land behind it, where they grazed their cow.

The nymph noticed that the farmer and his wife took great pleasure in the few violets that grew by the doorstep of their cottage. Each time, upon entering or leaving their home, they sniffed the blossoms to catch the modest fragrance that wafted up into the air.

"I shall give you a field full of the loveliest smelling violets that I can find," said the nymph. "But take care that you keep the flowers to yourselves."

Overnight, the meadow in back of the poor cottage was filled with a new kind of violet, with larger petals of velvety smoothness. Best of all, the flowers had a perfume unlike anything that existed before. The couple named the new flower "pansy," and took great delight in it.

But they could not resist showing it to their neighbors and friends. Soon, there were crowds of people trampling the meadow. Everyone rushed to exclaim over the beautiful flowers and to smell the enticing scent. They stamped down the grasses where the cow usually grazed. Soon there was nothing but bare earth surrounding the pansy plants and they began to get dusty and wilted.

The couple called on the nymph.

"I cannot take away a flower once it is growing," said the nymph. "But I can take away the smell." And she did.

Since that time, the pansy remains a lovely, velvety flower, but it has no fragrance at all.

THE SECRET STORY IN THE PANSY
European Folklore

The pansy has three multicolored petals and two plainer ones. Beneath the five petals there are four sepals. The central pistil or carpel is partly concealed by the showy corolla (set of petals). There are many variants of a story one can tell while holding a pansy blossom and gently pulling off the petals. This version combines elements found in German, Dutch, French, Danish, and Czech folklore. English versions usually tell of the fairy hiding in the pansy.

There was once a king who was of a retiring disposition. His wife and daughters, however, liked to live in comfort and wear beautiful things. The mother and two older daughters always wore gold and purple velvet gowns. *(Point to the three multicolored front petals.)*

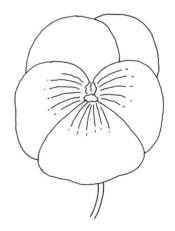

They each had a green velvet stool to sit upon. (Gently remove the three front petals, one by one, and show the three sepals on which they were resting.) The two younger girls wore plainer gowns, but still of velvet. *(Point to the remaining two petals.)*

They were small and had to share a stool. *(Gently pull off the two petals and show the one sepal on which they were resting.)*

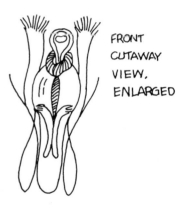

FRONT
CUTAWAY
VIEW,
ENLARGED

The king had often complained of the extravagance of his wife and daughters, but after they went away, he was sad and lonely. There he sits with his little round head bent, wearing the red tie his daughters gave him, and with his feet in a tub of warm butter to give him comfort. *(Carefully show the carpel as it rests in the calyx. The illustration shows the ''king'' as he might appear if the front part of the calyx were sliced away. A magnifying glass helps to show the detail of the stigma, the pollenic pore and the nectar lobes projecting into the spur. Note from the side illustration the position of the ''king'' in relation to the stem.)*

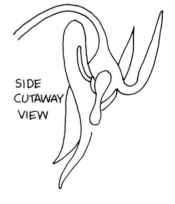

SIDE
CUTAWAY
VIEW

THE HEALING PLANT
Hungarian (Christian) Legend

A long time ago, the people of Hungary were suffering from many diseases. There seemed to be no cure for many of them. Ladislaus, their good and beloved king, was very concerned.

One night, in a dream, an angel told him to go into the forest and shoot off one of his arrows. This he did, and the arrow landed at the foot of a gentian plant. Ladislaus gave this plant to men and women who were healers. They used it in many ways to help those suffering from illness and pain. The gentian is still used today for some of its healing properties.

THE TREE OF RICHES
French and West Indian Legend

Several hundred years ago a Frenchman by the name of Charles Plumier became a botanist. The legend as to how this came about is probably not historically accurate, but it makes a lovely story.

Plumier decided he would like to travel the world and get rich. A fortune-teller told him: ''Search for a tree that grows near churches and graveyards; its blossoms are the color of the new moon; its fragrance will overpower your soul; if you uproot it, the leaves and flowers continue to grow. When you find it you shall be rich.''

Plumier traveled far and wide until at last he reached the West Indies. He went to an old woman known for her wisdom and described the tree that the fortune-teller had told him about.

''Do you know where such a tree is found?'' he asked the wise woman.

The old woman told him that she did indeed know of such a tree.

''You must go to the church near here, at midnight, on a full-moon night. There you will see a tree spreading its branches along the wall. Shake the branches and you will soon see riches beyond imagining.''

Plumier did as he was told. He found a small, lovely tree and shook it. Blossoms fell all around him, glistening like golden coins. The fragrance did overcome his soul, and he suddenly realized what real riches were: the calm beauty of the night, the sweet scent of the flowers, the peace of the churchyard. He stopped looking for material wealth and instead continued to look for wealth in nature, discovering many plants. The family of trees that he found was named ''plumeria'' after him. But some call it white jasmine or frangipani.

WHY CARROTS ARE THE COLOR OF FLAME
Wallonian Legend

Soon after the vegetable plants were created and put on the earth, the carrot, which had been planted in shallow ground and given a small round shape, was dissatisfied with its place. The carrot had heard that there was an interesting and forbidden place deep down inside the earth.

So the carrot began to stretch and stretch its root, pointing it further and deeper into the bowels of the earth. Some say the carrot root actually reached the gates of Hades, and stayed there for six months, deciding whether to stay or go back up. Its leafy stalks, which had once been low on the ground, began to stretch up and up, pulling on the root until it was close to the earth's surface.

But when the root was pulled up, it had turned a bright orange-red, from having come so close to the flames. And carrots have been that color ever since.

BERGAMOT
English Literary Tale

In the time when the hills were young, there was a girl who stood in her father's garden and nipped the leaves off a plant of bergamot. The fresh sharp smell of them rose up to her. At that moment, an old woman with a pack on her back appeared at the garden gate.

''Good day to you,'' said the lass.

"Good day, my child," said the old woman. "Is there anything you want in this pack of mine? It's all for sale."

The girl saw a little round pot.

"That is just the pot to hold my bergamot," she said, "but as for money, I have none."

"Tush!" said the old woman. "For your good will and a touch of your hand, you may have it and be welcome."

The girl stretched out her hand, but no sooner had she touched the pot than her fingers stuck fast, and she was forced to follow wherever the old woman led, over hill and hollow and bog and bramble, until they came to the dark forest.

The father and mother of the girl looked high and low for her, but they could not find her; so they sat by the fire and wept, and the house seemed to rattle around their ears, it was so empty without her. It so happened that a great war had just ended and one day, at sunset, a soldier came marching by the cottage.

"Do you have a soft spot on the floor and a crust of bread for the likes of me?" he asked.

The old people were as radiant as the sun on a spring morning to have a third person in the house again. The soldier was given the best of everything. In the morning he prepared to set off again.

"Is there anything I can do for you between this point and the end of the world?" he asked. "Because that's where I'm going."

The old couple made him sit down again and they told him all about their daughter: how one minute she had been picking bergamot, and the next she was gone as clean as if she had married the wind.

"Could you look for her?" they asked.

"If the earth stays dry and the sea stays wet, I shall find her for you," he answered, and with that he marched off without looking behind him.

He trudged through dry and dusty ways until he came to a thick forest. The soldier took out his sword and slashed a path as straight as the briars allowed. By and by he came to an open space. There was a great brick wall, higher than his head, without a sign of a door in it.

"It takes more than a wall to daunt me," he said, and knocked on the wall with the handle of his sword. The leaves rustled and the birds whistled but *the wall did not open*.

"Steel does not do it—let's try wood," said the soldier as he knocked on the wall with his walking stick. The leaves rustled and the birds whistled but the wall did not open.

"Neither steel nor wood does it—let's try flesh and blood," said the soldier as he spread his hand flat on the wall and laid four kisses in the spaces between the fingers.

Whish! There he was, inside the fairest garden he had ever seen. There was one of every flower and plant that the soldier had ever known, except one. He sniffed and sniffed, and finally knew what smell it was that he missed. There was no bergamot in that whole garden.

The soldier went on until he came to a little gray house at the farthest end of the garden. On the doorstep sat a girl with her hands in her lap.

"Good morning," said the soldier. "I'm thinking you're the one I'm looking for."

The girl just looked at him with eyes as blank and brown as the water in a well. She was certainly bewitched. So the soldier rapped at the door.

Out came an old woman.

"What do the likes of you want at my house?" she asked.

"I'm looking for a girl to help me through life, and this girl would do nicely," said the soldier.

"Oh, no. She is bound to me for several years," replied the old woman. "But you may have her if you can catch her. I'll give you three days to manage it."

It was agreed that he could make the first attempt on the following morning. Then they all went in to supper.

With the first bite that passed his tongue, the soldier knew that the meat had no salt in it. He had a bit of salt in his pouch and when the old woman was not looking, he sprinkled a pinch on his own plate, and then a good pinch on the food on the girl's plate.

When she took the next bite, she looked as though she were remembering an old name. When they got up from the table, the girl passed close to the soldier and whispered, without turning her head.

"A little brown rabbit is worth something."

The next morning the soldier ran downstairs as if the steps were hot iron instead of cold stone. But when he came to the courtyard, he saw nothing of the girl. He waited and fussed and fumed until at last he thought he saw something beyond the sweet williams. He stole over quietly and there was a little brown rabbit, with eyes as blank and brown as water in a well.

The soldier stooped to pick up the rabbit by the ears. Whoosh! Away it scampered with a whisk of its heels, and he went after it, through the roses and hollyhocks, through the cabbages and onions, and then through the wheat and barley, and into the dark forest. They ran all day, until the sun went down.

The soldier went back to the little gray house, and there was the girl sitting at the table as if nothing had happened. As they ate the soldier sprinkled salt on her meat as before, and when they got up from table, the girl brushed against him. When he looked at his jacket, there were three brown rabbit hairs on it.

The next day he ran as he had never run before, through the marigolds and mignonette, through the lettuce and carrots, and then through the rye and oats, and into the deep forest. But again he could not lay his hands on the little brown rabbit.

By this time the soldier realized what was happening. That night, instead of going back to the old woman's house, he trudged off through the deep forest and walked until he came to the cottage of the old couple, where bergamot grew in the garden.

"What do you want at this hour of the night?" asked the old man when he answered the soldier's knock.

"Three things," said the soldier. "The kettle hanging on a nail over the fire there, the mirror that hangs on the wall, and a handful of bergamot from your garden."

He got what he asked for and off he set before the sun was up. At the foot of an alder tree in the deep forest, he left the kettle. At the foot of an ash tree, he left the mirror. At the foot of an oak tree, he left the handful of bergamot. Then he set off for the little gray house. Nothing was to be seen but the little brown rabbit, slipping away through the lilies.

Off went the soldier after it. They ran through the peonies and lady's slippers, through the peas and turnips, and through the corn and millet, until they came into the deep forest. On and on they went, until the rabbit came to the alder tree, and saw the black kettle. She stopped for a heartbeat and murmured:

"There is the hearth kettle, That I have polished clean."

And the kettle answered:

"The nail is lonely where I hung, And the spit and the fire screen."

But the brown rabbit picked up her heels and ran faster. By and by she came to the ash tree and saw the mirror. She stopped and looked in it.

"There is mother's mirror, That might reflect a queen."

And the mirror answered:

"The wall is lonely where I hung, And the boards and cracks between."

The little brown rabbit looked at herself once more and the soldier was almost upon her. But she laid back her ears, and ran faster than ever. On and on they went until at last she came to the handful of bergamot. She stopped short.

"In the witch's garden, No plant like this have I seen."

And the bergamot answered:

"The birds are lonely where I grew, And the path and hedges green."

The brown rabbit sniffed at the green leaves. Then she cried in a voice of remembrance, "Bergamot!" and down she fell, stiff and still.

Up came the soldier, and when he saw the little rabbit lying as still as a stone, he scratched his head in dismay. Then he kneeled down beside her and looked between her ears. Sure enough, there he saw the sign of the old witch's skinny hand.

He cut off a silver button from his coat, a lock of his red hair, and twined these in a ball, together with a sprig of bergamot. He put the ball in his gun, took careful aim, and fired between the ears of the little brown rabbit.

Bang! There was no rabbit sitting beside him but a fresh-faced girl with eyes as brown and clear as the water that bubbles over stones in a mountain stream.

"Now we must go home," said the girl, "and the next time I shall not be tempted by a tramping peddler."

She stuck a sprig of bergamot in the soldier's cap, and they set off merrily, carrying the handful of bergamot, the mirror, and the kettle.

12

In good time they came to the cottage where the bergamot grew.

And if they were not married, it is a great shame, for a story without a wedding is like a peacock without a tail.

Adapted from Margery Bailey's *Seven Peas in the Pod*

THE TWO TREES OF PARADISE
Islamic Legend

There are two trees in Paradise. One is enormous and spreads over a vast area. It is covered with millions of leaves—one for each human being on earth. At the very moment a child is born, a new leaf bursts forth on the tree. And each time that a person dies, a leaf falls to the ground.

The second tree is also large. It covers the homes of the souls with shade and sends forth cooling breezes. Its branches are filled with fruits of every kind, and with fleeces and cotton and other things to make clothing. Those who need food or clothing have only to reach out for it.

WISE WORDS AND POPCORN FLOWERS
Mexican Custom

When the ancient Mexicans wished to show in a picture that someone was speaking "wise words" or "wisdom of the old ones" they painted flowers coming out of the mouth of the speaker. This meant the words were as beautiful and as precious as flowers.

Corn was considered a very sacred grain by the ancient Mexicans. For special feasts, corn kernels were heated and popped. The people called these popped kernels "flowers." They were not meant for eating, but for stringing into garlands and necklaces to be worn in honor of the gods.

Ornaments to Make

CREATING ADORNMENTS FROM COMMON FLOWERING PLANTS

Chains, Wreaths, Garlands, Necklaces, and Bracelets

Method One—For Flexible Stems
Cut the stems off at a point approximately three inches (eight centimeters) below the blossoms. Place the second flower slightly below the first flower.

Twist the stem of the first flower up and around the blossom of the second flower as shown. Hold in place while you reach for the third flower.

Place the third flower in line with the first two and twist the stem of the second flower up and around the blossom. Continue adding flowers in this manner until you have the length you wish.

To form a wreath or circlet, simply take the stem of the last flower added and bring it gently up and around the blossom of the first flower.

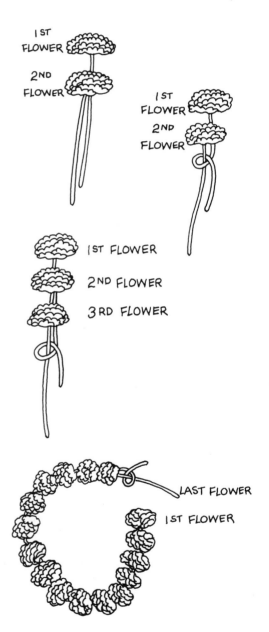

Method Two—For Nonflexible Stems

Cut the stems off at a point approximately two inches (five centimeters) below the blossoms. With the sharp tip of a pocket knife, make a slit midway along the stem of the first flower. Slip the stem of the second flower through the slit and pull until the stem is completely through and the blossom is resting on the stem of the first flower.

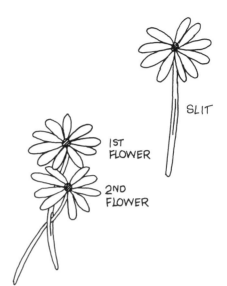

Make a slit in the second stem and add a third flower. Continue until you have the length you wish.

To form a wreath or circlet, work the stem of the last flower gently into the same slit on the first flower that holds the stem of the second flower.

Method Three—For Long, Thin-Stemmed Plants

Select plants with stems at least a foot long. These can be flowering plants or plants with bushy heads of seeds or grains. Kentucky blue grass, wool grass, daisies, fleabane, Queen Anne's lace, cow parsnips, yarrow, and coneflowers are among the many common weeds or plants that can be used in this method.

Strip off most of the leaves from the plants. Start with three plants that have stems of varying lengths. Braid the three stems, beginning just below the plant heads. When you come toward the end of the shortest stem, place another plant with the head just *above* the point where the braid is to be continued, with the stem parallel to the short stem end. Continue braiding and adding plants as you come to the end of each stem.

When you have achieved the length you want for a wreath or necklace, stop adding plants, braid the three stems as far as possible and wind the remaining stem ends around the bottom of the braid to hold it closed.

Gently flex braid into a circle and tuck the tied end under the head of the first three plants where you started braiding.

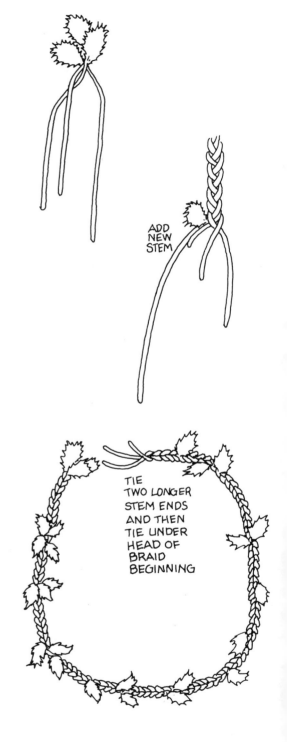

ADD NEW STEM

TIE TWO LONGER STEM ENDS AND THEN TIE UNDER HEAD OF BRAID BEGINNING

16

Method Four—For Long, Thick-Stemmed Plants

Cut off as long a stem as possible. Slit the stem down the middle or cut it in a notched pattern, almost up to the point where the blossom begins. Tie or twist the two ends gently around your wrist or neck.

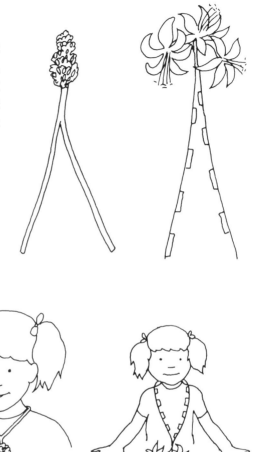

Rings

Small circlets can be made from violets, pansies, and other small flowers by cutting a small slit at the point where the stem joins the sepals (where the petals are held together), and then slipping the tip of the stem through the slit.

"Wedding" Rings or Chains

Select dandelion stems that are long and smooth. For finger rings, cut off segments three inches (eight centimeters) long; for chains, use stem segments four to five inches (ten to thirteen centimeters) long. Work the narrower end into the wider one, forming a ring.

To make a chain, simply slip a stem through the ring before forming the next ring.

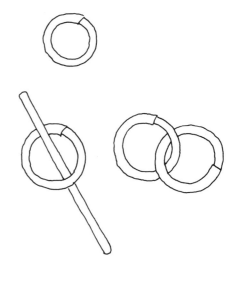

Fingertip Covers

Slip blossoms such as foxglove, bluebell, beardtongue, Canterbury bell, mullein, or snapdragon over the tip of each finger.

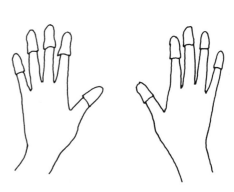

Earrings or Ear Decorations

Make a large dandelion stem ring with a small ring attached (see above). Slip the large ring over the ear so that the small ring hangs down from the lobe.

Or slip a double cherry stem over each ear, making sure the cherries come to rest near the ear lobes.

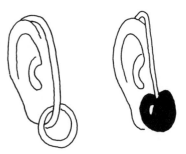

Hair Ornaments

Select a stalk of field grass that has an interesting placement of leaves in relation to the stem. Cut off the stem about eight inches (twenty centimeters) from the top and tuck it into your hair, either straight up or sideways.

In Japan, children like to do this with a stalk of the plant, because it reminds them of the traditional hair ornaments worn by grown-ups when their hair is fixed in the elaborate coiffures of olden days.

If you find a small birch tree that has fallen, peel off the curly first layer of birch bark and wrap some of the curls around clusters of your hair, like barrettes.

Often, wild grape vines or dodder plants are strangling another plant or tree and you wish to remove them. You have then found the right moment to play old-fashioned hairdresser.

When cutting away the twisty vines, save the parts of the stem that are like corkscrews. Leaves may be stripped off or left on, depending on the effect you wish to create.

DODDER
PLANT
TWINED
AROUND
CLOVER

19

Wind the curly stems around strands or bunches of hair on someone's head. Try to make the longest curls possible.

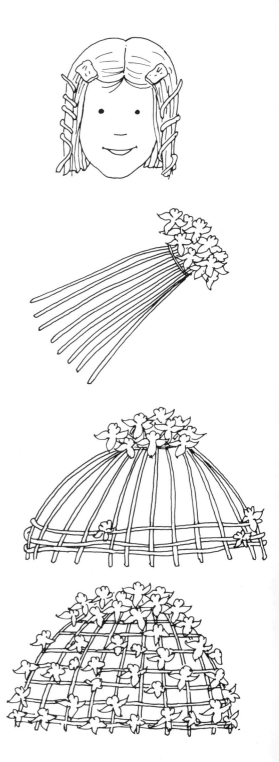

Flower Cap

Gather a bunch of gentians (garden variety, not wild) or other long-stemmed flowers in which the blossoms are at the top and the stems relatively free of leaves. Lightly twine a stem or vine around the top of the bunch, under the blossom heads, to hold them in place.

Separate the stems by placing them over a post or plastic bowl, so they make a caplike shape.

Weave at least two rows of stems around the bottom edge of the cap, going over and under in alternating pattern. This will help the cap hold its shape. If you prefer, start at the top and weave the entire cap in rows from top to bottom. It will be more stable. Pick up frangipani, jasmine, or other sweet-smelling blossoms that have fallen to the ground. Tuck them in all over the cap.

PART TWO

Disguises

Almost everyone likes to hide occasionally. Disguises are a means of concealing our identity by putting on wigs, masks, mustaches, glasses, false noses, or other fakery.

It is fun to play a game of disguises using only natural objects to cover and conceal. The game can be played purely for the fun of it, or an element of competition or contest can be added.

While walking along with one or more companions, try on a fern mustache or a leaf mask. Search for seeds, grasses, branches, or other objects that can be held to the face or head and then admire or giggle at the effect.

One or more of the following stories can be shared while meandering along.

Stories to Tell

WHY PLANTS NO LONGER GROW AS HIGH AS THE SKY
Chinese Legend

A long time ago, many plants and trees grew as tall as the sky. Their top leaves and branches poked into the heavens. People had been warned to stay away from the heavens for they were watched over by a fierce group of demons.

But there was a gang of mischievous children who liked nothing better than to climb tall trees and swing on long vines. One day they climbed right up to the sky, and continued their fun by jumping from cloud to cloud, playing pranks on the guardian demons. The sky echoed with their teasing laughter.

The demons began to chase the children back down. In their rush to get to earth safely, they tore off bark and leaves and branches. This made the trees and plants very unhappy, and since that time, they grow up toward the sky, but they never reach for the heavens.

THE CREATION OF PLANTS
Jewish Legend

On the third day God created the plants—the earthly plants as well as those in Paradise. First of all He made the cedars of Lebanon and the other great trees. In their pride at having been put first, the trees shot up high into the air. They considered themselves the favorites.

Then God spoke: "I hate arrogance and pride, for I alone am exalted and none besides."

So God created iron on the same day. It was the substance with which trees could be cut down.

The trees began to weep. When God asked the reason for their tears, they said: "We cry because you have created iron to cut us down. All the while we thought we were the highest of the earth, and now you have called iron, our destroyer, into existence."

God replied: "Without your assistance the iron will not be able to do a thing against you, for you yourselves will furnish the axe with its handle."

Then God gave a command to the trees to bear seeds after their kind, and to multiply. After this, He created the grasses, but He gave no such command to them.

So the grasses said to one another: "If God had not desired all living plants to be divided into classes, He would not have instructed the trees to bear seeds after their own kind, especially since the trees seem inclined of their own accord to divide themselves into species."

Then the grasses decided, by themselves, to reproduce themselves also, after their own kind, and to spread out over the earth.

When God saw this, He exclaimed: "Let the Glory of the Lord endure forever; let the Lord rejoice in his works."

WHY SOME LEAVES ARE SHAPED LIKE THE HUMAN HAND
Persian and Flemish Legend

The first human pair grew up as a double tree. Each half had branches that spread over the places in the opposite half where the ears and eyes eventually developed. When the double tree reached maturity it was separated into two by divine decree. Each half was endowed with a separate existence and a human soul. At last, the crown was transformed into two human heads with the gift of knowledge. The branches became arms and legs.

Some other trees wished to be thus transformed and they managed to change part of their shape. But in the end they remained trees. However, their leaves have stayed in the shape of the human hand, as a sign that humans are descended from trees.

OVERHEARD IN A VINEYARD
Arab Legend

Kumeyl, son of Ziyad, was very clever and quick-witted. At the time he lived, long, long, ago, there was a leader who was very mean-spirited. Kumeyl did not approve of his conduct, and often spoke against him in secret. One day, while standing in the vineyard of an acquaintance, he spoke harshly of the leader.

The man heard about it and called Kumeyl to him.

"You must be banished," he said. "You are no longer welcome here."

"Why?" asked Kumeyl.

"It has been reported that recently you said that my face should turn dark with shame; that my head should be cut off at the neck; and that my blood should flow purple-red."

Kumeyl came up with a quick reply.

"It is true I said those things. I was standing at the time in a vineyard. First I spoke about you. Then I noticed a huge bunch of green grapes. I exhorted them to blush for shame at being still so green in the warmth of the sun. And then I wished that they would be ready for me to cut off at the neck, so I could enjoy the delicious flow of their blood-red juice."

This explanation calmed the leader and Kumeyl was allowed to continue living there in peace.

THE HIDING HAZELNUTS
French (Christian) Folklore

In olden days shepherds picked long, leafy branches of hazelnut trees in spring. They held these up or tied them around their faces to make disguises. Then, on White Friday (nine days before Easter) they went to church and tried to fool their sweethearts. The branches were blessed and after the leaves had dried and fallen off, the shepherds used the sticks to prod and guide their sheep for the remainder of the year. The next spring they repeated the process.

WHY TREES WHISPER
Estonian Legend

In the early days of earth, not long after the trees were created and humans were forced to leave Paradise to work, a man went out to the forest to cut wood. The first tree he came to was a pine tree. But as soon as the man lifted his axe he heard a voice cry out.

"Don't strike me. Can't you see the sticky tears that are already coming out of my body? If you hit me it will bring you bad luck."

The man did indeed see the sticky sap coming from several cuts in the tree trunk, so he moved on farther into the forest. He came to a spruce tree and again raised his axe. But the spruce tree protested.

"Don't cut me down. You will find me of little use for my wood is twisted and knotty."

Unhappily, the man went on until he came to an alder tree. Once more he raised his axe to strike but the alder shrieked at him.

"Be careful that you don't wound me. Whenever I am cut, blood runs from my heart. It will stain my wood and your axe blood red."

The man went no further but called out to God.

"How am I to get wood to make fire and to build shelter? Every tree I meet cries out and pleads that I not cut it down."

God took pity on the man and said: "Return to the forest. I will see that henceforth no tree will talk back or contradict you."

The man did as he was told and this time no tree spoke to him. None protested as he cut them down to make shelter and to make a fire.

The trees were not happy about this. They dared not complain aloud against God. Instead, they began to whisper softly, each time a person entered their domain in the forests. If you approach a group of trees anywhere, you can still hear them softly whispering to each other. They are gently complaining about their poor treatment at the hands of humans.

THE WILD WOMAN OF THE BIRCH WOOD
Czech Legend

A shepherdess sat at the edge of a grove of birch trees, guarding her flock. As she sat, she spun flax into linen thread.

Suddenly there appeared before her a strange woman dressed in a filmy garment of white. She had long, flowing hair and on her head she wore a crown of wildflowers.

"Do you like to dance?" the woman in white asked the girl.

"I'd like to dance the whole day," answered the shepherdess. "But my mother has given me all this flax to spin."

"Tomorrow is another day," said the woman.

"Yes, I can spin tomorrow," thought the girl. So she jumped up and the two began to dance.

They whirled wildly, but so lightly that the grass under their feet was neither trampled nor bent and the sheep gazed in wonder.

When evening came, the girl guided the flock home but said nothing to her mother. The next day she took her flock to the same birch grove. She sat down with the pile of flax, determined to spin it all.

But again the woman in white appeared.

"Will you dance?" she asked.

"I cannot," said the girl. "I must spin all day. Today my mother will surely ask about the flax."

"I will help you spin, if only you dance with me," said the woman. Once again they twirled and leaped in a madly joyful dance that lasted most of the day. Then the woman waved her arms and lo and behold! the flax was spun into fine linen thread.

The girl returned home and gave the thread to her mother but said not a word.

For the third day the shepherdess returned with her flock to the birch grove. There waited the woman in white.

They danced as never before, skimming over the grass as gently as wind-whirled leaves. At the end of the day the woman spun the flax and then she reached out to the branches of a birch tree. She gathered some golden birch leaves and put them in the pockets of the shepherdess's apron.

"You have pleased me with your dancing," she said and then disappeared.

When the girl returned home she gave the linen thread to her mother and this time her mother looked at it carefully.

"Where did you get this? Surely you did not spin it?"

The shepherdess then told of all that had happened the last three days.

"It was the wild woman of the birch wood!" exclaimed her mother.

"She said my dancing pleased her and she gave me these birch leaves," said the girl with a laugh. But when she emptied her pockets her laughter turned to silent wonder, for the leaves were of solid gold.

WHY CORN HAS SILKY WHITE HAIR
Southern United States Tale

Once there was an old man who never did see fit to think that one day he was goin' to die.

One day Old Man was on the porch in his rockin' chair and he see someone walkin' up the path to the house. "Evenin'," he called out, "you a stranger 'round here?"

"Evenin' Old Man," the stranger say. "No, I ain't no real stranger 'round here. Come through this way every once in a while. My name is Death."

When Old Man hear that, he stop rockin'. "Well, evenin', Death. Didn't expect you. You got business 'round here?"

"Funny how lots of folks don't expect me," Death say. "Yes, I am on business, Old Man. I come for you. Put on your hat and let's go."

Old Man he didn't want to go. He liked it fine where he was. He say, "Yes, sir, Death, thank you kindly. Mighty fine of you comin' all this way. But I sure could use a little more time. I got a big field of corn out there to take care of. Maybe you could stop by again in two-three weeks?"

"Well," Death say, "go tend your corn, and I'll be back next Saturday." Death went off elsewhere.

Three-four days went by, and on Saturday mornin' the old man was in the cornfield pullin' weeds. He heard the cornstalks rustlin', and Death was standin' there. "Well, come on, Old Man," Death say, "I'm real busy this mornin' and I can't stand around."

"Good mornin', Death," Old Man say. "It's a fine mornin'. This dew on the ground makes it good for pullin' weeds. How'd you like to give me a hand?"

Death got kind of mad when he hear that. "Now look here, Old Man, I ain't no field hand. I got my own work to do. I got a regular schedule to fill."

"Death," Old Man say, "I wonder can you give me a little more time? Folks has a big need for corn, you know, and this field needs lots of attention."

"All right, then," Death say, "get on with your weedin'. I'll pick you up next turn around."

"You do that," Old Man say, "just drop in next time you're in the neighborhood." When Death went away, the old man went back to weedin' the corn field. Fact that Death kept comin' back didn't make no impression on him. He didn't do nothin' to get ready, just went ahead like he always did. Winter went past and the old man forgot all about Death. But he was beginnin' to feel mighty poorly. His rheumatism was gettin' worse. His eyes was gettin' more dim, and he didn't hear so good.

Next spring Death came along. "Come on, Old Man," he say, "it's time."

"Mornin', Death," Old Man say. "Have a chair and rest yourself."

"Now, look here, Old Man," Death say, "I'm real busy and you foolin' me. Put on your hat and come on."

Old Man didn't want to go along this time any more'n last time. "Tell you what," he say, "I'm mighty sorry to see you makin' all these trips, and I'm goin' to make it easy for you. You just get on with your work, and next time you figure you need me you can send me a sign and I'll come. Save you a lot of walkin'."

"What kind of sign?" Death ask him.

"A sign I can see or a sign I can hear," Old Man say, "either one. That'll give me time to get this corn crop sowed."

"That's a promise, ain't it?" Death say.

"It's a promise," Old Man tell him, "in the name of the Good Book."

"All right then," Death say. "When you hear the sign or see the sign, just put on your hat and come on."

"So long," Old Man say.

Old Man was mighty old by then. He got to feelin' more and more poorly. His eyes got dimmer and his ears got weaker, and in two-three months he couldn't neither see nor hear a thing. He was deaf and blind.

One mornin' a letter come. It was a sign from Death. But the Old Man couldn't read it, 'cause he was blind. Four-five days later Death sent a messenger to tell the old man: "Death sent me to give you the sign to hear." But the old man couldn't hear a word, so he didn't put on his hat and go.

So Death came himself. He looked and saw the old man was deaf and blind and couldn't neither see a sign nor hear it. He was mad. "You fooled me, Old Man," he say. "I'm not comin back no more."

The old man got more poorly all the time, but he didn't die, 'cause Death had passed him by. His beard got longer and scragglier all the time, and he wasted away till there wasn't hardly nothin' to him. He kept tendin' his corn, but he couldn't see where he was goin' and got to fallin' and tanglin' up with the stalks. He got so thin and poorly one day he just disappeared altogether.

But if you look on the corn ears you can see that there's some white hair hangin' on the ends. That's some of the Old Man's whiskers he lost whilst fallin' around 'mongst the cornstalks.

Folks say he never did die, just disappeared.

THE POWER OF FERNS
Cornish Legend

Jenny Permuen was a young girl who set off one day to look for a place to work. At the junction of four crossroads, she sat down on a boulder and thoughtlessly began to break off beautiful fronds of ferns that were growing all around.

Suddenly a man appeared before her and addressed her by name.

"Jenny, why are you here, pulling at these ferns?"

"I'm on my way to the market town," she replied. "I wish to obtain work. I only stopped here to rest."

The man said he was a widower with a little son.

"I am in need of a woman to help care for my boy. I like your looks, Jenny. I will engage you here and now and I promise to pay you well, but I require that you swear an oath. You must kiss one of those fern fronds in your hand and repeat after me: For a year and a day, I promise to stay."

Jenny was charmed and flattered. She had visions of a beautiful house in which to work. Without hesitation she took the oath.

The stranger set off eastward, and she followed him. They walked on and on until Jenny grew weary and lay down. She closed her eyes.

The man took a bunch of ferns and passed them over Jenny's eyes. Her weariness disappeared like magic.

They walked a bit further and soon Jenny found herself in fairyland. The man's house was all she had dreamed it would be. The young son delighted her. She went about her work singing and smiling.

She worked for her allotted time of a year and a day and then, one morning, on waking, Jenny found herself asleep in her own bed in her mother's cottage.

OIL PALM AND RAFFIA PALM
Nkundo (Zaire) Dilemma Tale

One day, when the trees were having a feast, Oil Palm and Raffia Palm began to argue.

Oil Palm said: "I am more important than you. From my fruit, humans get many nourishing things to eat. They press oil from my fruit and nuts, and use it to cook, or to rub on their bodies. With my sap, I supply them with palm wine, which they enjoy very much. Some of my curved branches make excellent bows with which to hunt, so humans can have meat. Other branches they use as brooms to clean their houses. As soon as my fronds and flower stalks are dry, people burn them and from the ashes they make salt to flavor their food. And when I am finally cut down, people take my core and eat it as a delicacy in salad."

Raffia Palm replied: "I am as important as you. People pull out my inner strands and soak them; they pound them until they are thin and then weave them into clothing. Some of the strands they make into ropes, to snare animals. With other strands they weave sleeping mats. My fronds are used to cover their roofs, and they make better brooms than yours, because they are longer and stronger. My flower stalks are also burned, so that the people can make salt from the ashes."

Dilemma: Which is more important, Oil Palm or Raffia Palm?

Some of the Nkundo say that at the time Oil Palm and Raffia Palm got to this point in their argument, a person passing by was asked to be judge of their case. The judge, when he had heard both statements, said: ''Oil Palm is more important than Raffia Palm, because he is the source of more food for humans.'' Raffia Palm was very angry when he heard this. ''Give back the clothing you now wear, made from my raffia. And never again will you be permitted to wear clothing.'' The judge was forced to flee into the bush and become a chimpanzee.

Others say it is Raffia Palm that is more important, because humans can always find food elsewhere. But who else will give them, for nothing, material to make clothing, a home, and a place to sleep?

What do you think?

TWO RIDDLES
Lithuanian and Flemish Folklore

A one-legged woman wears
One hundred dresses.
    Lithuanian folklore

She has only one foot
And she carries her heart in her head.
    Flemish folklore

Answer to both: A cabbage

WHY PLANTS HAVE HUMAN CHARACTERISTICS
Iroquoian Myth

Before the earth was created there was a land above the sky. Certain beings, men and women with human characteristics but not entirely human, lived among the sky people. These beings grew so numerous that the land above the sky became crowded. The beings began to quarrel among themselves and with the sky people.

The sky people went to the Great One and asked: "Can you not do something to bring back peace to this land above the sky?"

The Great One poked a hole in the sky and blew his breath through the hole, so strongly that a cloud of mists formed in the space below. He then asked the sun to shine through the hole. When the sun's rays fell on the mists, they turned to water and formed a great sea.

Then the Great One called the Moon and asked her to shine through the hole. As she shone down, a thick scum formed on the sea. Gradually, the scum drew together into a solid mass and made the earth, with the sea all around it.

Great One now had a place to send the beings, but when he saw how bare the earth was, he decided he must first change some of the beings into plants and animals, and send them to all the corners of the earth.

So Great One changed most of the beings into plants and animals, and then with a great breath, scattered them over the earth. And that is why every living thing on earth has some human characteristic, because each kept one thing from the time when the beings lived in the land above the sky. In animals it is easier to see these characteristics, but if one looks carefully, they are to be found in plants as well. Some plants have leaves shaped like the human hand, or like an eye or ear. Some have hair that looks like human hair. Others have flowers shaped like faces or feet. All of them, whether in an open or a secret place, have one thing that shows they are also descended from the beings in the sky, just like humans.

Disguises to Make

PLAYING A GAME OF DISGUISES
WITH NATURAL MATERIALS

Put together a large pile of old shirts, pants, dresses, nightgowns, or other cover-up types of garments that are washable. Each participant or group selects an outfit (or set of outfits). Do this in secret, or at different times, if the participants decide they would like to try to fool the other participants and onlookers. In such a case, each participant or group will need a large plastic bag in which to store the outfits until they are needed.

Agree upon a time limit and a boundary limit if there is access to large farms or fields or forests. Indicate which cultivated plants are not to be touched.

If there is a group of twenty or more, of mixed ages, who wish to be active participants, have them divide up into teams of one adult and one child. Those who have plant allergies or who prefer not to be disguisers can be the judges or the audience at the end.

The one absolute rule is that all of the disguise elements (other than the clothes) must be natural and must be placed or held on the body without the aid of pins, clips, glue, tape, or any other manufactured means.

Give the participants a suggested list of things to watch for, such as blown-down branches of trees, ferns, corn silk, birch bark, vines, fallen seed pods, large-leaved weeds, and the like. Show the participants the pages that follow, giving suggestions for disguising the hair and face. If they look carefully, they will surely see other possibilities.

One to two hours is usually sufficient for locating good disguise material. Many of the plant materials wither if kept longer than that.

Select a convenient gathering point and have each participant or group agree on a nearby spot each will use as a secret "dressing room." Make sure the "dressing rooms" are far enough away from the gathering point to be concealed completely from each other and yet close enough to enable the participants to walk to the gathering point while holding on to the various elements of disguise.

Have the nondisguised participants be the judges. If you wish, award prizes for the most imaginative disguise, the most effective one, and the most elaborate one. If you prefer a noncompetitive version, simply have all participants come to the gathering place at the same time, and enjoy each other's efforts.

Wigs and Head Coverings

Pick out small leafy branches that have fallen to the ground or that can be cut off with no harm to the tree or bush. Place the branches in your hair in such a way that they cover the entire head.

Select a group of thick ferns and carefully cut off about ten fronds. Arrange them with the stems hooked into your hair and the tips falling to your shoulders. Place one or two thick fronds over the top of your head.

Save the long, silky hair from at least a dozen cobs of corn. Twist or braid the blunt ends of two small bunches, and drape over your head, leaving the curly tips hanging down on either side. Continue until your head is covered.

Watch out for small birch trees that have fallen but are not yet completely decayed. Or look for bark that has fallen from large birch trees. Peel off the birch "paper" in curls and wrap the curls around bunches of your hair until your head is completely covered. (This will work best on someone with short hair.)

Look for dodder plants or vines that are twisted around other plants or trees. As mentioned in the section on Hair Ornaments on page 19, cut away the very twisty portions and twine them around your hair, making corkscrew curls. Keep as many leaves intact as possible to hide the color of your hair.

Mustaches and Beards

Select a plant with a long fuzzy top, such as pigeon grass or squirreltail grass. With the tip of a penknife blade, carefully split the stem down the middle, a little more than halfway into the fuzzy top. Place the two split sides on your upper lip, leaving the uncut part hanging down like a small beard.

You can also do this with a fern frond, for a lacy green beard.

Select a wide, long leaf from a corn plant. Use tree sap, milkweed juice, liquid from corn kernels, or other natural juice or sap to "glue" the leaf in place on your chin. Make sure it is something safe for your skin and that you are not allergic to it.

Place a maple bud on your upper lip and hold it in position by curling the lip a bit.

A leaflet from a fern frond will also work as a mustache.

For a larger mustache, locate two milkweed pods that are side by side, and just ready to open. Hold them in place with the upper lip.

Select several milkweed pods that are open, with the white silky floss ready to fly away. Cut or twist open a milkweed stalk and dab the juice on to your chin. Quickly attach pieces of milkweed floss. Continue until your chin and jaws are covered to your satisfaction.

Face Makeup

Crush berries until juicy and rub them against the cheeks. Or use half of a juicy red beet. Be sure to use only berries, fruits, and vegetables that are safe to eat, and keep the juice away from the eyes.

Masks

See if you can find a leafy branch that has eye openings placed just right for you. Hold it up in front of your face.

Select a large leaf from plants such as burdock or rhubarb. With your fingers or your pocket knife, carefully punch eyeholes. Hold the leaf up in front of your face.

Select two approximately equal lanceolate leaves, such as lily of the valley or tulip. Make sure the stems are long and intact.

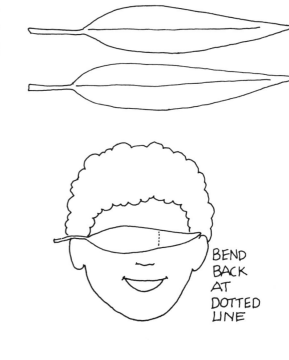

Hold one leaf up loosely over the left eye, placing stem over the left ear. Fold back the tip of the leaf one inch (two and a half centimeters) beyond the point where it reaches the bridge of the nose. Then, with your fingers, mark the spot where the eyehole should be and, taking the leaf away from your eye, tear or cut out eyehole.

BEND BACK AT DOTTED LINE

Place the second leaf back to back with the first leaf and cut or tear an eyehole in it. Bend back the tip on the second leaf at the same point as the bend in the first leaf. Cut or tear off the leaf tips.

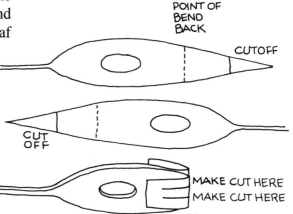

POINT OF BEND BACK

CUTOFF

CUT OFF

MAKE CUT HERE
MAKE CUT HERE

Place the leaves back to back again, with torn-off ends on the outside. Make two cuts or tears in the folded-back leaf segments, as in diagram.

MAKE SURE CUTS ARE THROUGH ALL 4 THICKNESSES

Fold back the central cut segments.

Select two thin-stemmed, smaller lanceolate leaves, such as thin willow leaves for a graceful effect or colored leaves for a more variegated effect. Certain flowers or grasses will also give interesting results. Weave them, crisscross, through the upper and lower folded-over leaf ends. Make sure one stem goes through the top folded-over leaf end and then through the bottom folded-under leaf-end; the second stem must go through the top folded-under leaf-end and the bottom folded-over leaf-end.

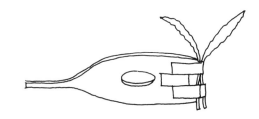

Carefully open up the leaf mask and place it over eyes, pushing stem ends gently into hair over ears, as though they were eyeglass frames. If you have thick, bushy hair above your ears, this will work beautifully.

Find a large birch tree that has fallen in the woods, with the inner, woody part already soft and decayed. Select a piece of the trunk that is relatively round and intact and large enough to fit over your head. Clean out all the remaining inner pulp. Set the bark shell in the sun a few minutes to dry. Look for a segment that already has interesting shaped openings for the eyes, or tear out the openings in whatever shapes you wish. Use tufts of fluffy milkweed for eyebrows.

If you cannot find a decayed birch trunk still retaining its fully round shape, cut off squares or rectangles of bark and make masks that you can attach to your head with vines or reeds. Decorate the masks with interesting seed pods for the nose. Or weave in grass fronds to suggest an intriguing hair arrangement.

Birch bark can often be stripped or scraped or pulled apart to use the clean, inner surface. But the outer surface with its unusual natural designs usually provides the more interesting possibilities. Remember to use only fallen birch trunks. Stripping the bark from living birch trees can harm them.

Palm Tree Leaf-End Masks

When a branch falls from a palm tree, the end part often dries out in a form that makes a perfect mask shape. In the Ivory Coast one can see beautifully decorated masks of this type, looking like a colorful herd of elephants. Susan Patron, a California librarian who grew up in Hollywood, remembers that she and her friends often played with masks made from fallen palm branches.

To make such a face covering, cut off a fallen palm branch at approximately the point where the fronds begin. Poke two eyeholes or slits in appropriate places and hold the mask in front of your face.

If you wish to simulate an elephant's head and trunk, select a larger branch that has been curved downward by the weight of the fronds. Cut off lower down on the stem. Carefully tear or break away some pieces along the sides to simulate elephant ears. If necessary, hold the ears in place by stacking weights in the appropriate positions until the leaf is dry and holds its shape on its own.

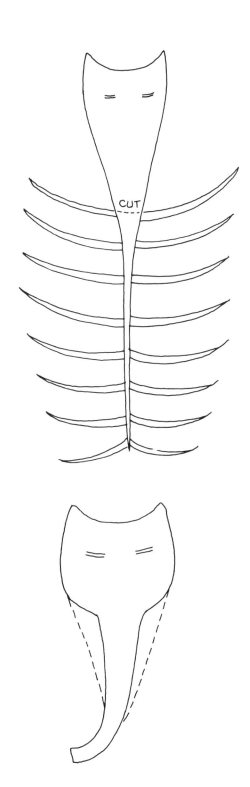

Whole-Body Coverings

Select wild grape or large dodder vines or other plants that must be cut away or pruned. Twine them around yourself or ask a friend or family member to do it. Arrange airy vines and leaves around your head. Move slowly across the ground. You will appear to be a walking wood spirit!

Put aside an old sheet or blanket to cover two persons. Select plant parts that can disguise you as animal forms. For example, to be an elephant, select two large floppy leaves (burdock are excellent) for ears and one smaller leaf for the head. Braid grasses for the trunk and attach them to the head leaf. Curl up leaves for tusks and attach with vines to the ear leaves. Then attach all to the head of the first person, using vines. The second person bends over the first person and arranges the sheet or blanket to cover both bodies. For a tail, the second person can hold in the correct spot a stalk of any plant with a bushy or fuzzy white top, such as pipewort, devil's bit, or the like.

PART THREE

Playthings

Simple toys made out of things found in almost any park, meadow, or garden can give just as much pleasure as the most complex manufactured playthings. As you walk along, be on the lookout for hollow-stemmed plants, long smooth leaves, old dried corncobs, feathers that have fallen from birds' wings, and other items that look as though they might be fun to play with. The best kinds of toys to make are those that take no more than five minutes to construct. Follow the instructions given later, or invent playthings on your own.

These are some of the stories you can tell as you go on your searches for the materials.

Stories to Tell

THE FAIRY CLOCK
Irish Folklore

In Ireland, they say, when fairies dance in the meadows of a moonlit night, they must be careful to disappear before dawn or they will be seen by humans and lose some of their power. So they delegate a leprechaun to blow the down of dandelions at frequent intervals, to tell them how many hours are left until dawn. The number of seeds left after blowing hard three times tells the hour.

And that is why, even today, some Irish children still try to tell time by blowing three times on dandelion puffs.

THE TOY CANOES

Hawaiian Tale

Tell this to your father on Father's Day

A long time ago, there was a King of Kauai who had six sons. The eldest decided to go out and seek his fortune.

After a long time, he had still not returned. His family was sad. The King turned to his other five sons and said, "One of you must go and search for your brother."

"Let me go!" cried out each of the five brothers.

The King then said, "The one I send must be very clever. I shall give you all a test, so I can decide which of you to send."

He ordered them each to make a toy canoe from the leaf of the ti plant. When the canoes were ready, he took his five sons down to the sea and waded with them into the water, until the waves came up to their thighs. Then he said, "Now put your toy canoes in the water and blow them on their way."

His sons did as they were told. The four oldest blew and blew until their canoes were far out to sea, as though they were going in search of their oldest brother.

But the youngest son blew his canoe toward his father until it bumped right into his father's legs.

"It is to you that our brother must come back," said the youngest, as he kept blowing the canoe in a circle around his father.

The King chose the youngest son to go off in search of his brother.

THE LEAF HILLS OF TIMOR

Malay Folklore

On the island of Timor, in the Malay archipelago, travelers used to fan themselves with leafy branches. When they had rested and cooled off, the travelers threw the branches on one of the particular spots marked off at the side of the road, and continued on their way. They believed that their fatigue was left behind in the discarded branch.

Generations of travelers passed along many of Timor's roads and even today one can find in some places the huge hills of leaves where they have thrown off their tiredness after a short rest and a cooling breeze from a fan made of a leafy branch.

WHY SOME REEDS ARE HOLLOW
Thai (Buddhist) Myth

Once the Buddha-that-was-to-be was reborn as the king of the monkeys. He lived in the forest with his eighty thousand monkey followers. One day, the monkey followers came to the bank of a deep pool where they had never been before. They were thirsty but instead of going near the pool to drink, they waited for the Monkey King to arrive.

As the Monkey King drew near, he looked down at the ground. Then he circled the pool, all the while looking down at the footsteps on the banks. He noticed that there were many footprints going down to the water, but none coming back.

He realized, then, that the pool must be haunted by an Ogre.

"You did well not to go and quench your thirst before I arrived," said the Monkey King to his followers.

When the Ogre noticed that the monkeys were not coming up to the pool, he called out to the Monkey King, "Why do you not approach the water's edge?"

"Because we know better," the Monkey King called in reply. "You are surely waiting there to pounce on one of us the moment we get close to the water."

"Well, I shall have you sooner or later," said the Ogre fiercely, "for there is no other fresh water nearby, and you must drink to live."

"We shall see about that," said the Monkey King. He glanced around and saw a bunch of tall reeds growing in the marshy areas next to the pond.

"Bring me one of those reeds," he requested one of his followers.

As soon as he had the reed in hand, the Monkey King recited a prayer and blew down into the reed stalk. It became hollow, without a single knot left in all its length. He went up and down the marshy area, causing all the reeds to become hollow.

Then the Monkey King picked up his reed, extended one end until it touched the water, and put the other end to his mouth. He sucked in his breath and soon he was drinking the cool, clear water from the pool.

"Now each of you must do likewise," the Monkey King told his followers.

Using the long, hollow reeds, the monkeys drank their fill. The Ogre furiously swirled the water in the pond, but there was nothing he could do. He did not succeed in catching a single monkey.

And ever since then, many reeds have been hollow. We can still use them as drinking straws.

AN OLD RIDDLE

Portuguese, Spanish, and French Folklore

Sleeper slept. Hanger hung on. Comer came on. Do you know who they are? Here are some clues.

If Hanger who hung on had not fallen on Sleeper who slept, Sleeper who slept would have been eaten by Comer who came on.

Answer: Sleeper is Pig; Hanger is Acorn; Comer is Wolf.

MONKEY MONEY

Parisian Tale

There was once a beggar who went about with a pair of monkeys. He came to the gates of Paris but was not allowed in because he had no money to pay the tax that was customary in those days.

The beggar began to sing and the monkeys began to dance and act silly. Soon the officer in charge of the gate as well as all the people standing around were laughing and enjoying the monkey's antics.

The beggar gave a few walnuts to the monkeys to reward them for their dancing. The monkeys cracked the walnuts, ate the nut meats, and then walked up to the officer in charge of the gate and handed him the empty walnut shells.

The officer laughed merrily and let the beggar and his monkeys pass into Paris. Since that time you will occasionally hear people refer to empty walnut shells as "monkey money," and to try to get in to some place without paying the fee is called "paying with monkey money."

LITTLE COCK AND LITTLE HEN
Dutch Folklore

The area around peony bushes is a favorite place for roosters and chickens to peck for worms and ants and seeds. Some say the reason this bushy plant is so thick with foliage is that it was once used as a hiding place.

Little Cock and Little Hen were pecking away near a peony bush when a fox approached at a distance. The rooster and the hen went to hide under the bush, pulling the leaves all around themselves to hide their feathers. The fox was fooled and went on his way.

From that day on, the peony bush stayed rounded and full of glossy green leaves. And in the flower heads are hidden the remnants of Little Cock and Little Hen. Take a peony blossom that is fading and gently strip off all the petals. If you look carefully, you can see Little Cock and Little Hen, sitting on the calyx.

MONDAMIN
Algonquian Legend

It was a time of great famine and Manabozho wanted to bring relief to his people. So he made a leafy shelter deep in the forest, and there he prepared to spend days and nights in fasting and prayers.

On the fourth day, at sunset, out of nowhere there appeared a young man dressed in green garments; his long silky hair was yellow and on top of his head he wore a set of plumes.

"Come and wrestle with me," he called to Manabozho.

47

Manabozho was weak from lack of food but something told him it was important to answer the call, so he came out of his leafy tent.

"I am Mondamin," the tall, shining young man said.

As they wrestled, Manabozho noticed that his strength was coming back. He could hold his own with the stranger.

The sun went down and Mondamin said: "Enough. I will come again tomorrow at the same time."

They wrestled again on the following day, the fifth day of Manabozho's fast. On the sixth day, Mondamin came again.

"Your prayers have been heard," he said to Manabozho. "You have proven your courage. Tonight, wrestle with me for the last time, and then overcome me. After that, bury me here in the soft earth where sun and rain can reach me. Let no weeds grow on my grave, and protect me from the raven."

Manabozho did all he was told. Mondamin lay sleeping, through rain and sunshine. Manabozho kept the weeds and birds away.

One day, a small green plant pushed through the soft earth. It grew and grew until there was a tall stalk of shining green, with silky tresses and plumes on its head.

"It is Mondamin," said Manabozho, as he shared this gift of corn with all his people.

THE TULIP BED

Devon (England) Legend

Near a pixie field there lived an old woman who possessed a cottage and a very pretty garden. There she cultivated a most beautiful bed of tulips. The pixies so delighted in this spot that they carried their elfin babies there, put them inside the tulips, and sang them to sleep. The delicate music would float in the air and the beautiful tulips waved their heads to the evening breezes. It almost seemed as though they were keeping time to the music. As soon as the elfin babies were lulled asleep the pixies would return to the neighboring field, and there they began their dancing. They danced all night in the fairy ring, but at the first light of dawn they returned to the tulips. After kissing and caressing their babies, they took them home.

The old woman tended the bed of tulips with extra care, and never let even one of the blooms be plucked. The pixies rewarded all this attention by allowing the tulips to bloom longer than any of the other flowers in the garden. And they were surrounded by a perfume more fragrant than the roses.

But at length the old woman died. The new owners of the cottage removed the bed of tulips and planted parsley instead. But the parsley withered, and even in the other beds of the garden nothing ever grew well.

And so the people of Devon say: Before you remove a bed of tulips, check to see if they have a fragrance, and watch to see if they last longer than the other flowers. If they do, then it is better to leave them be, for they might be pixie cradles.

LILY OF THE VALLEY

Medieval European (Christian) Legend and Korean Folklore

Sometimes the hero of this legend is Saint Leonard. In Korea, it is a friendly giant who conquers the dragon.

A long time ago, Saint Leonard walked up and down the land, proving his great power. One day, he climbed a mountain, wanting only to find a quiet place to rest. He reached a place where no human foot had trod and where the forest was so thick that for a thousand years the sunshine had not penetrated it. There he lay down, with a rock for his pillow and leaves for cover.

But he soon discovered that he would not be able to rest, for he had entered the home of a fierce dragon. The dragon came lumbering up, its eyes sending daggers of light and its scales shining like a coat of steel. The fire spurted out of his nostrils and mouth, setting the grass and trees aflame where he breathed on them.

But Saint Leonard was not afraid. He fought as he had never fought before, twisting and turning and attacking the dragon from all sides.

The struggle was long and fierce but at last the dragon's fire was quenched and he fell to the ground, dead.

Saint Leonard was weary and his victory had not been without pain. Bruised and bleeding, he descended the mountain into the valley. Wherever he stepped, the grass and flowers were trampled, but in the spots where his drops of blood fell, new green growth appeared. Each drop of blood changed into a crystal, and from the crystals there sprang up sprays of lily of the valley. Around the delicate flowers there grew thick clumps of leaves, shaped like the blade of Saint Leonard's sword.

NINE PEAS IN THE POD
Belgian and French Custom

As you prepare to cook some fresh peas, open up each pod carefully and count the peas inside. If there are nine peas in any of the pods, put them aside. Cook them separately and serve them to the one you love. During the following year you will marry that person.

THE KING OF THE TREES
Old Testament

The trees went out once to anoint a king over them. They said to the olive tree, "You reign over us."

But the olive tree replied, "Should I leave my rich oil, which God and humans honor in me, just to go waving to and fro over the other trees?"

So the trees said to the fig tree, "You come reign over us."

The fig tree answered, "Should I leave my sweetness and my good fruit just to go and wave to and fro over the other trees?"

Then the trees said to the grape vine, "You come and reign over us."

The grape vine said, "Should I leave my wine, which God and humans find cheer in, and go to wave my fronds to and fro over the trees?"

Then all the trees said to the thorn bush, "You reign over us."

The thorn bush answered, "If you really want to make me king over you, then you must all come and live in my shade."

But the thorn bush had almost no shade, and because it was so dry, it easily caught fire, and devoured the trees, even the great cedars of Lebanon.

Adapted from Judges 9:8–15

Playthings to Make

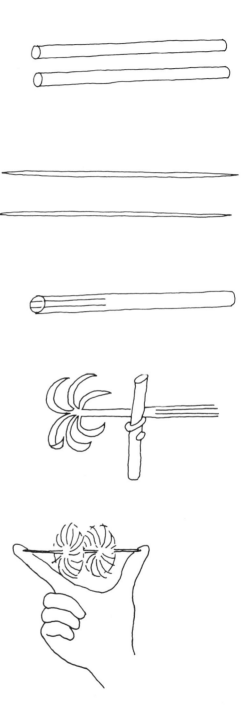

MAKING TOYS FROM PLANTS

Dandelion Stem Spinners

Select the fattest stems of several dandelion plants. Cut off lengths of stem about three to four inches (seven to ten centimeters) long. Smooth out some twigs so that they are about the size and shape of toothpicks, with no rough edges. (You might even cheat a little and use toothpicks!)

Make two or three slits through one end of a dandelion stem. Using a round branch the size of a pencil, roll back the stem ends one by one, as though you were setting curls. Do the same on the opposite end of the stem.

Slide the smooth twig (or toothpick) through the hollow stem and then blow on your spinner. Or hold it up into the wind to see if you can find out in which direction the breeze is blowing.

Henbit Spinners

Locate a henbit plant (lamium amplex-icaule or lamium album). Cut off a piece of the stem that includes two leaf whorls.

Locate a thorn from a hawthorn tree, or smooth out a thin twig (or cheat a little and use a toothpick).

Stick the thorn or twig through the middle of the henbit stem, at the exact midpoint between the leaf whorls. Hold the thorn horizontally and blow on the upper leaf whorl.

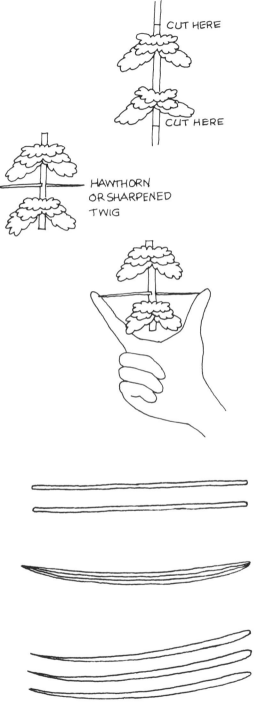

Leaf Ducks or Swans

Select a group of narrow bladelike leaves, from plants such as cattails, sedges, irises, or the like. They should be at least two feet (sixty centimeters) long.

While you are searching for the leaves, also try to locate long stems of reeds or canes that are hollow, or with a soft pith that can be easily removed to make them hollow.

Strip one leaf into long, thin strands to use as ties.

Bend one of the leaf ends as shown in the illustration. For ducks, have the head stick up two inches (five centimeters) and for swans, three inches (eight centimeters).

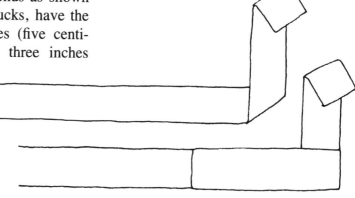

Make a rectangular shape, bending the leaf at each corner. Continue winding the leaf around and around, until it is approximately the size of a sardine tin. Always bend the corners so they stay in position.

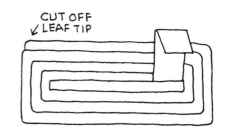

CUT OFF
LEAF TIP

When you have reached the desired size, cut off the leaf tip just at the point where it reaches one of the corners on the long side of the rectangle. Then tie the figure, toward the back end, leaving the ends of the leaf strip sticking up like a tail.

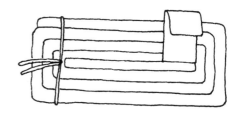

After you have made several figures, put them in the water and watch them float. Blow into a long reed aimed at the flock, and send them scurrying over the water.

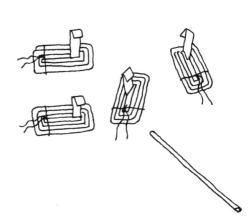

Whirlybirds

Dried corncobs have many uses. When properly dried, they can fuel a roaring campfire. Yet those same corncobs can be made into a type of pipe that some smokers enjoy. They also serve well as objects for play. The whirlybird is an easy toy to make and provides hours of fun.

Select a well-dried corncob. It must be one on which the corn kernels grew to maturity, not a corncob from the variety that is eaten.

Search for three wing feathers that birds have shed on the ground. They should be approximately six to eight inches (fifteen to twenty centimeters).

Break off the wide base of the corncob so that you have about five to six inches (thirteen to fifteen centimeters) left. Poke the feather quills into the soft middle part of the corncob. Angle the feathers outward, in a triangle, equidistant from each other.

Now your whirlybird is ready to test. Throw it into the air as high as you can. It should twirl and whirl as it descends. You may have to make some adjustments in the placement of the feathers, or in the length of the cob, but with practice you will be able to make it perform just right.

Leaf Boats

This is good to try when you have a bed or bunch of tulips on which the blossoms are gone; or you can wait until it is time to thin out the leaves in a thick clump of lily of the valley; or search for wild plants that grow in abundance and have leaves of this shape.

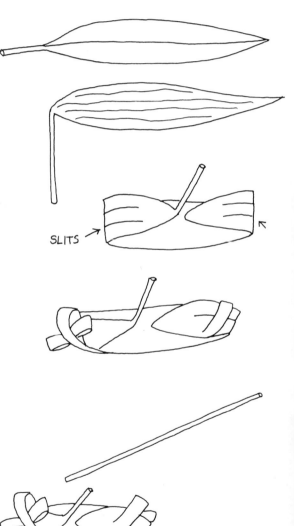

Select tulip or lily of the valley leaves (or similar ones) that are at least eight inches (twenty centimeters) long. If they are longer, so much the better. Leave a bit of the stem attached to each leaf.

Fold back each leaf end approximately two inches (five centimeters). Make two slits at each end, as indicated in illustration. Weave the end strips into each other, as shown.

SLITS

Put the leaf boat on water, and watch it float. To make it sail away, blow on it through a long, hollow reed.

Stilts

The thrill of walking along at a height above everyone else around seems to be a sensation that appeals universally. Stilts have been made for centuries, and in many parts of the world.

One of the best times to make a set of stilts is after a walk through a forest where there are many fallen branches.

Search for two fallen branches that are straight and about two feet (sixty centimeters) taller than you are. They should be no thicker than what you can circle comfortably with your hands. At the thicker end, they must have a crook where a smaller (but sturdy) branch is or was attached. Break off all but eight inches (twenty centimeters) of this smaller branch. Then break off all other twigs and branches and peel off any old bark so that the main branch is as smooth as possible. You should end up with two almost straight branches, each with a V at about the same distance (one foot or thirty centimeters) from the lower end.

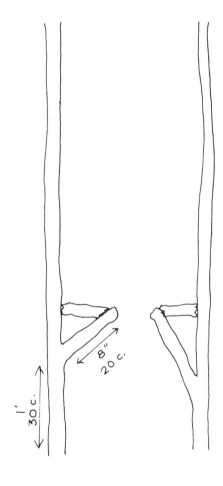

Now break off two pieces of a dead branch to lengths that will fit inside the V's, as crosspieces. You may have to whittle a bit to make the notches so that the crosspieces fit snugly.

Your stilts are now ready to use.

Leafy Tent

After many summer storms one awakens to find numerous large branches of trees blown down on the ground, or half hanging. Sadly, there are even whole trees that do not survive some storms. The best one can do is to pick up the pieces and use them for firewood, after drying. Sometimes, branches can be gotten from a tree service company that is doing heavy pruning.

When there are quite a number of large blown-down branches (or some cut down because of required pruning), select about six to ten of them that are at least eight feet (two and a half meters) long. If they are longer the tent can be roomier. However, they must be approximately the same length. Trim off projecting smaller branches on one side of each of the large branches, except for any small offshoots near the broken-off end. Lay the branches in a circle, trimmed side downward, in the spot where you intend to set up the tent.

With the help of a tall friend and a stump or something sturdy to stand on, begin to set up the tent by propping up the branches, with their leafy tips at the bottom and the broken-off branch ends at the top. Find the best way to lean the broken-off ends against each other, and twine any small offshoots at that end around and under, like rope. Continue until you have a complete circle, and all the large branches are resting against each other, with the topmost offshoots wound in and around to hold everything firmly into place.

Weave the small leafy branches that you tore off into the spots on the outside of your tent where there are gaps.

Enjoy your leafy tent for as long as it lasts.

Pea-Pod Canoes

When you are shelling a batch of fresh peas, put aside the fattest, longest pods. Shell them last, by carefully slitting open the straight side, and leaving the curved, lower side intact.

SPLIT THIS EDGE

Take out the peas and prop open the pods with two twigs no longer than three quarters of an inch (two centimeters). Use one twig at each end.

VIEW LOOKING DOWN FROM ABOVE

Place the pea-pod canoe on water and watch it float, or blow on it through a straw or reed. Make an entire flotilla of pea-pod canoes.

PART FOUR

Dolls for a Day

Dolls have been made by humans for at least fifty centuries. Most of the early ones were made of wood, clay, or metal. Some people have made dolls out of leaves, fruits, and other parts of plants, but they have often required several hours of concentrated work. Many dolls are so loved that they are kept for a long time.

The dolls suggested here should each take only a few minutes to construct, and they will last only a day or even less. They are meant to be made entirely of natural things. The pieces should be held together by branches, twigs, thorns, grasses or strips of bark. They should stand up on their own, if possible, or at least be able to be placed upright in a table crack, or some other convenient spot.

If a group of people wish to make dolls at the same time, you may decide to set aside a time and area limit (as in the "Disguises" section, pages 33–42). At the end, you could have a judging. Try to determine which is the most beautiful doll, which the most unusual, which uses materials in the most ingenious manner, which is the most amusing, and so on. Each participant who makes a doll may vote.

If you prefer a completely noncompetitive activity, simply have a doll show, so that everyone can admire the results of imagination at play.

The ideas shown here are just to get you started. If you look well as you walk along, you will soon see parts of dolls in almost everything around you. Watch especially for such things as apples and other fruits that have fallen to the ground and have interesting spots for face markings; galls on stems of weeds; leaves of all sizes and shapes; plants with bushy, flowery heads that can be tipped upside down for use as skirts;

milkweed pods and seed pods of all types; oats or tree fungus of interesting shapes; thorn and thistle branches; ears of corn; grasses and plants with leaves placed as for arms and feet.

While searching for your doll materials you might tell some of these stories, since they are about many of the plants for which you are looking.

Stories to Tell

THOR'S MANTLE
Norse Folklore

Thor was the Norse god of thunder and lightning.

In the Nordic countries, after a summer storm, the plants grow very quickly. The burdock's leaves grow so large and wide, one leaf will sometimes cover a man's shoulders. And so, in those countries, the burdock is called Thor's Mantle, because it is big enough to cover the shoulders of the tallest and strongest of the gods.

THE THORN BUSH, THE BAT, AND THE DIVER
European Fable

A thorn bush, a bat, and a diving bird became friends and decided to go into business together. The bat borrowed money and made it available for the trio to buy a boat to start up their search for trade.

The thorn bush brought a handsome set of clothing for each of them, so that they could appear prosperous, as all business owners should.

The diver came up with some nuggets of gold to trade for things that they would later sell at a higher price.

And so they sailed off. But soon, a tremendous storm swelled the sea and shook their boat so strongly that they lost everything, except their lives.

They reached the shore but ever since then the bat flies about only at night for fear that the moneylenders will see him and ask for their money back.

The diver continues to wade in the water at the edge of the land, searching with his beak for the pebbles of gold.

But the thorn bush went out into the countryside and there he stayed. He grabs at the clothing of every passerby to see if it is one of the fine garments he had contributed to the business.

MR. BUTTERFLY AND HIS FLOWERS
Japanese (Buddhist) Tale

There was a man who lived in a suburb of Miyako and who never married, but devoted himself to cultivating the flowers in his garden. Besides the flowers he had no other companion than his old mother. No one knew his name, but he was known as Mr. Butterfly. When his mother died he was left alone among his flowers. They added to his melancholy, for they faded and withered. It grieved him to see them die when the frosts of autumn came. One evening as he looked about his garden and listened to the sound of the temple bells that rang out through the dusky twilight, he decided to abandon the world.

He became a hermit and went to live among the mountains far from any town. For a long time he was completely alone and had no visitors. But one night there was a knocking at his gate. He went out and found there an old lady dressed in deep blue robes. She asked him to preach to her. The hermit hesitated at first to let her in, but on second thought, he decided it was safe.

While she sat and listened to him, out of the mist there suddenly appeared a young lady dressed in willow green and wearing a purple mantle. She came in and sat down quietly beside the older woman. Then more ladies appeared, one after another. Some had pale yellow dresses, others wore white or pink. One was covered by a white and purple gown of silk. Finally the congregation became a group of thirty women, young and old, each dressed in beautiful clothes of varied shades. They all listened attentively to the hermit's sermon.

The hermit did not know what to make of all this, but he went on with his sermon. He emphasized the vanity of a worldly life.

"Do we not all—humans, plants, and beasts alike—come to the same final destiny?" he concluded. After he had finished speaking the women expressed their appreciation and confessed that in reality they were the spirits of the flowers he had loved.

"We came in order to share your spiritual attainment," they whispered. Each of them left a poem, which was an expression of gratitude as well as a confession of faith.

As the last of them disappeared, the morning dawned; the grasses and bushes that grew around the hermitage quivered softly in the morning air and sparkled with new-fallen dew.

"Now I know that all living things are destined to become Enlightened Ones," said the hermit. And for the rest of his life he stayed there, living in simplicity and holiness.

POMONA AND VERTUMNIS
Roman Myth

A pome is a fruit consisting of sweet, juicy flesh surrounding a core containing seeds. Apples, pears, and quinces are pomes. The word comes from Latin, the original language of this myth.

Pomona was a wood nymph but she did not care for the forests and rivers. Instead, she loved gardens and cultivated fruit trees, especially those that bore delicious apples. She spent her time pruning and grafting and taking care that her favorite trees would never suffer from drought. She diverted streams of water to their thirsty roots.

She kept her orchard gates locked and allowed no men to enter. She was so lovely the fauns and satyrs would have given all they possessed to win her, and so would old Sylvanus, and Pan. But the one who loved her best of all was Vertumnis. He used every trick he could think of, trying to get near her to plead his cause. Once he disguised himself as a reaper, carrying corn in his basket and wearing a band of hay around his head. Another time he pretended to be a cattle herder. On still another occasion he carried a pruning hook and ladder and appeared ready to work among the apple trees. Each time he managed to catch glimpses of her, but he was never able to approach her closely.

One day, he disguised himself as an old woman, with a cap covering gray hair and a long staff to lean on. Vertumnis thus entered Pomona's garden and admired the fruit. And then he kissed Pomona—not exactly like an old woman!

He spoke to her in these words: "If you are prudent and will let an old woman advise you, pay no heed to any suitors except Vertumnis. I know him as well as he knows himself. He is not a wandering god, but belongs to these hills. Nor is he like so many lovers today, who love anyone they happen to see. He loves you and you only. Moreover, he loves the same things that you do and delights in gardening. He would handle your apple trees with great care. Take pity on him. Pretend that it is he speaking through my mouth. And remember that Venus hates a hard heart. Do you not know how she turned a noble lady into a statue of stone because the lady mocked and laughed at the young man who loved her?"

When Vertumnis had finished his impassioned speech he dropped the disguise of the old woman and stood before Pomona in his proper form, as a handsome youth, radiantly alive and bursting with love. He appeared to her like the sun breaking through a cloud.

He was ready to renew his pleas, but there was no need. His eloquence had won her heart. Her orchards from then on were watched over by two gardeners. And the apples took on the fresh rosy-cheeked looks of the two handsome caretakers, Pomona and Vertumnis.

CANTERBURY BELLS
English Folklore

In the cathedral at Canterbury in England is a shrine to Saint Thomas à Becket. Many people liked to come to the shrine to pray to Saint Thomas. In those olden days, they came on foot or on horseback. Many of the pilgrims' horses had small bells attached to their harnesses.

When there appeared a pretty, bell-like flower in the meadows of England, the people thought it looked like the bells on the horses of the Canterbury pilgrims. So they named the flowers Canterbury bells.

HUMANS FROM CORN
Quiché (Guatemala) Myth

When the Life Givers first made humans, they chose clay and water as the materials from which to make them. But the result of that was humans who were weak and watery. At the first signs of heavy rains or floods, they seemed to wash away.

Next the Life Givers made a man from the outer wood of trees, and a woman from the pith at the very center of the wood. Then the earth was filled with humans who were fine and straight-looking. But they were also hard and unbending, and constantly bashing each other. The Life Givers were still not satisfied.

Finally the Life Givers took ears of white and yellow corn and from them they formed humans who were supple and strong. They gave the humans long, silky hair just like the ears of corn. At last, the Life Givers were pleased with their creation and so they made these corn humans the ancestors of all the Quiché people.

THE TREE AND THE UGLY CHILD
Tagana (Ivory Coast) Legend

There was once a child who had a head full of wisdom and a heart full of love, but he was so ugly to look at that his parents thought they could not bear to live with him any longer. So they took the child deep into the rain forest and abandoned him there.

The child played for a time and then he found an unusual nut. The nut seemed to have a face and figure. Instead of eating it, the boy planted the nut in the ground. Before long, it grew up into a small tree.

The boy stood by the tree and called out:

> "Grow, my fine tree!
> Grow fruits for me!"

And the tree grew until it was covered with delicious fruit that the boy could eat.

Some time later the mother came back to the spot where she had abandoned her child and was amazed to see the tall tree standing there, filled with its luscious-looking fruit. She decided to climb the tree to pick some of the fruit.

At that moment her child, who was hiding nearby, called out softly:

> "Grow my fine tree!
> Grow so high she can't get free!"

The tree began to shoot up into the sky. It grew so quickly the mother was afraid to descend. She waited there until her husband came looking for her.

"Where are you, wife?" he cried out.

"I am here, husband, up in the top branches of the tree. I am afraid to come down."

The husband fashioned a special sling of reeds and vines and with it he climbed up the tree. As soon as he had reached his wife, their child called out from his hiding place:

> "Grow my fine tree!
> Grow as high as I can see!"

The tree shot up so high in the sky it was impossible for the husband and wife to come down.

"Please help us," they cried to their child. "Forgive us. We are sorry we abandoned you."

So the boy called out:

> "Shrivel and sink, my fine tree!
> Bend so low, my parents can see me."

The tree sank downward and the husband and wife were reunited with their child.

Ever since that time, parents in that part of the world never abandon their children.

KOUKIL

Ukrainian Legend

When God named and distributed the plants, the devil was absent. Afterward, he complained and whined.

"Even I should be allowed to be in charge of at least one plant," said the devil.

God took pity on him and said: "Very well. Remember this name—oats. Go to the Great Recorder and let it be put down that I have put you in charge of oats."

So the devil set off, saying over and over to himself: "Oats, oats, oats." But as he passed by a forest he heard a bird calling out: "Koukil, koukil, koukil."

The devil forgot what he had been saying and began to repeat over and over: "Koukil, koukil, koukil." And that is what he said when he came to the Great Recorder. So instead of being put in charge of oats, he was given charge of koukil, the flowerlike fungus that grows on oats.

MORAVIAN RIDDLE

Stoji v poli hůlka;	In the field stands a stick;
Na té hůlky kulka;	On the stick stands a ball;
A v té kulce	In the ball live children
Na tisice.	up to a thousand.

Answer: A poppy

Dolls to Make

MAKING DOLLS FROM PLANT MATERIALS

Miniature Flower Doll

Head: daisy
Arms: rolled leaf
Body: Canterbury bell
Underskirt: petunia

Roll up a leaf that is a few inches (eight to ten centimeters) long. Make a hole in the central part of the leaf and poke a small daisy stem through the hole. Put the stem through the hole in the bottom of the Canterbury bell. Poke the stem through the center of a large petunia.

Rhubarb Recluse

Head: rhubarb seed pod
Covering: rhubarb leaves

Cut off a rhubarb seed pod that looks like a wizened face. Leave about six to eight inches (fifteen to twenty centimeters) of stem attached, to use as a body. Drape rhubarb leaves around body with top side in. Fold over the upper part of the leaves to make a cowl.

Corn and Apple Doll

Head: apple
Hat: corn husk
Hair: corn silk
Arms: rolled corn husk
Body: corn with husks still on

Select a cob of corn with some of the stem still attached. Save the curved part of one leaf where it joins the stem, for the bonnet. Leave most of the husks on, and carefully open them at the top, gently putting the corn silk to the side. Cut or break off the tip of the corn. Poke one end of a sharpened twig into a windfall apple. Poke the other end into the rolled corn husk and then down into the middle of the corn cob. Arrange husks around the neck like a ruff. Bring the corn silk up around the apple on back and two sides and arrange like hair. Put on the bonnet and keep in place with thorns.

BREAK OR CUT OFF TIP

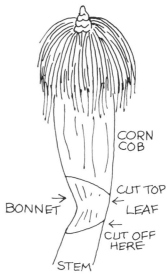

CORN COB

BONNET →

CUT TOP LEAF ←

← CUT OFF HERE

STEM

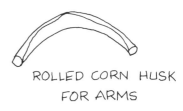

ROLLED CORN HUSK FOR ARMS

THORN

SIDEVIEW

69

Snowball Flower Girl

Head: gall on stem
Body and skirt: any flowering weed with
  bushy, branched-out blossoms.
Cape: large leaf
Bouquet: Snowball
Hat: Petunia

Poke a stem with a gall on it into the
middle of a bushy plant that has been
placed upside down. Bring leaf around
shoulders and overlap edges. Poke
snowball stem through overlapped
edges. Put petunia on gall.

Milkweed Devil

Head: milkweed pod
Body: large leaf
Legs: two milkweed pods
Tail: curly vine

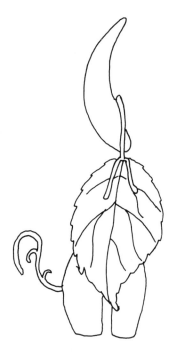

Find a stem on which two milkweed
pods are arranged close enough to each
other to pass for legs. Locate another
stem with an unopened milkweed pod
for the head. Poke both stems through
a leaf. Arrange the vine as though it
were a tail.

Dancer

Head: small snowball
Hat: petunia
Arms and upper body: three leaves on
  a stem
Upper skirt: two leaves
Lower skirt: leafy branch

Twine snowball stem, upper leaf stem, and lower leaf stem around each other and then stick into the center of a leafy branch. Arrange leaves so they fall in correct positions. Place petunia on snowball head.

Grass Elf

Head: acorn
Hat: flower petal
Body, arms, and legs: grasses

Poke a hole into an acorn shell. Find a sturdy grass stem and put one end into the hole in the acorn. Tie another grass stem just under the acorn head. Place a petal on the acorn.

Poppy Doll

This is a very old figure. Madame de Genlis, a French educator of the early nineteenth century, recommended games such as this to teach children an appreciation of the variety of plants and their parts.

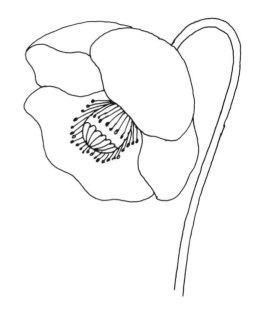

Pull or cut off a poppy, making sure the stem remains at least 5 inches (13 centimeters) long. Carefully bend down the front and back petals and tie them in the middle with a blade of grass or vine tendril, to make a waistline, as shown. This will be the dress.

Bend the side petals slightly downward, and roll them gently into armlike shapes. Tie at each end with grass or vine tendrils. Arrange so they are in arm positions. The field poppy has only four petals, in which case one petal is used for each arm. Garden poppies often have eight petals, in which case you may have to use four for the skirt and two for each of the arms.

The carpel, or seed pod, is the doll's head. Arrange it so the upper part looks like a skull cap and the lower part like the face. The stamens will form a ruff or collar around the head.

Ballerina

Head: crab apple
Upper body and arms: twig and grasses
Ballet skirt: tree fungus
Legs: twigs

Locate a tree fungus shaped like a bell skirt, with interesting markings. Search for two twigs that look like legs with shoes. Sharpen the ends of the twigs and poke them into the underside of the fungus. Locate a fatter twig and sharpen both ends. Poke one end into a crab apple and the other into the upper side of the fungus. Drape grasses around shoulders and down to skirt. Hold in place with thorns.

PART FIVE

Musical Instruments

Many of our musical instruments are made of natural materials, but they have been refined to such a high degree that it is difficult to find the natural object behind all the polish. Also, we forget that music often imitates natural sounds in the environment: the brushing of leaves against each other; the wind whistling through trees or rocks; the songs of birds; the snap, crackle, and pop of growing and dying trees and plants.

It is challenging to see what range of sounds one can come up with using only natural things, without altering them in any way. While searching for some "instruments" with which to make music or do rhythmic exercises, you might like to tell these stories.

Stories to Tell

WHY MOST TREES AND PLANTS HAVE FLAT LEAVES
Polynesian Legend

A long time ago the sky was not very high above the earth. It was the plants that held up the sky, pressing it outward as far as they could. But that was only a short distance from the ground, not even as high as the treetops.

The sky was very heavy, and the weight of it caused the leaves of

74

the plants to flatten out more and more. Some, like the leaves of the banana plant, spread into long thick blades as they pressed against the sky. Others, like the taro plants, became as round and broad as elephants' ears as they stretched out to hold the ever-expanding sky.

"We cannot hold out much longer," said the plants. "Soon the sky will fall and crush the earth."

"We must call for help," said the people.

"I will go to Maui," said a woman. "Maui is a trickster, but he is also wise and knows how to do many things."

"Yes, I can raise the sky," said Maui. "But first, you must give me a drink of water from your gourd."

The woman gave him a drink of water and Maui held up his arms. With his broad brown hands he lifted the sky until it came to the treetops. There he let it rest for a time, and the sky flattened the leaves of the trees.

Maui heaved his shoulders, raised his arms, and pushed again.

Soon the sky was resting on the mountaintops.

After he had rested enough, Maui made a mighty effort and hoisted the sky so high it reached the heavens, where it has remained ever since. But the leaves have remained flat, to show that they once held up the sky.

THE TREE OF LIFE
Mordvinian (Siberia) Legend

Deep, deep in the heart of a forest is a high hill. On that hill there grows a giant birch tree. The roots of that birch tree spread out underground so that they ring the earth and the branches surround the heavens. The leaves of the birch are the size of a giant's hand and the buds are as long as the lash of a whip.

At the base of the birch tree is a spring, roofed over with carved boards and white sheets of birch paper. On the edge of the board roof is a birch-wood container. In the container is a ladle of silvery birch bark. On the bottom of the ladle is carved a decoration of the sun and the moon. As the sun moves in the heavens, the ladle turns with it.

They say that if you fill the container from the spring, then dip the ladle into the liquid and drink deeply, you will live forever, for you will have drunk the water of life.

THE GIFTS TO THE FIVE NATIONS
Iroquoian Legend

The beautiful land of Akanishionegy was bright with rivers and lakes, but was without inhabitants. One of the gods, having raised it from the waters, and beholding its beauty, decided to make humans to dwell there. He came to earth and sowed five handful of seeds upon it. The seeds became worms, into which spirits entered, and they were changed into children. Nine years he nourished these children; nine more he taught them all manner of useful knowledge.

The children grew up and became the five nations. The god knew his work was finished. He called the five nations together to hear his parting words. Then he gave them each a last gift. To the brave Mohawks he gave corn; to the patient Oneidas, the nuts and fruits of the trees; to the industrious Senecas, he handed beans and other plants in pods; the friendly Cayugas received the root vegetables; for the wise and eloquent Onandagas he spread out squashes and grapes and other plants that grow on creeping vines.

Then the god wrapped himself in a bright cloud and went like a swift arrow to the sun.

THE GOURD AND THE PINE TREE
Persian Fable

Once, in the hot summer sunshine, a gourd began to stretch and twine itself around a fat pine tree. Swiftly the gourd plant grew, twisting and turning until it came to the very top of the tree.

"Look at me!" cried the gourd. "In less than a hundred days I have reached as high as you, but it took you more than a hundred years to get this tall.''

The pine tree murmured in answer, ''Yes, I have passed through the heat of a hundred summers and have borne the cold of a hundred winters in order to reach this lofty height. But I know I shall still be here this winter, whereas the first cold frost will bring you down.''

And just as the pine tree predicted, when the cold weather came, the vines of the gourd plant shriveled and shrank and fell to the ground.

THE GIANT PUMPKIN
Indian Legend

Long, long ago in India there lived a man named Iaia who had an only child, a son. The son died and the father did not wish to bury him for he could not believe that his child was gone.

So Iaia hollowed out an enormous pumpkin and took it to a mountain nearby. Then he placed his son inside the pumpkin, filled it with water, and covered it with the pumpkin top. Every day he visited the pumpkin and looked inside.

One day, he took off the lid and saw that it was full of little fishes, swimming in the water.

''The seeds have turned into fish,'' said Iaia.

Just then he saw something big come swooping out of the water. Quickly he slid the cover on to the pumpkin again.

''Could it be my son?'' thought Iaia excitedly.

He went home and began to talk about it with his neighbors.

Now there were four young men, brothers born on the same day, who were passing by the village that day, and they heard what Iaia said. They rushed off and went to the mountain in search of the giant pumpkin.

When they came to it, one of them opened the top and they saw all the fish swimming inside. The brothers decided to carry the pumpkin off, so they would have fish to eat whenever they wished. They lifted the pumpkin up to their shoulders and began to walk down the mountain.

But Iaia was so excited about having seen the living creatures inside the pumpkin, that he, too, decided to return to it. When the four brothers saw Iaia coming up the path, they got so frightened, they dropped the pumpkin.

The water gushed out and went tumbling down into the valleys, taking the fish along with it. There, it formed the ocean. And Iaia's son was borne along with it also, and has lived in its depths ever since, as the great whale.

FIRST FRUITS OF THE FIELD
Kabyle (North Africa) Legend

First Man and First Woman wandered around under the earth. One day they found a pile of wheat in a corner, and next to that a pile of barley. In other corners they found piles of seeds and grains of all kinds that are good to eat or to season food.

"What does this mean?" they wondered.

Near the wheat and barley ran an ant. First Parents saw the ant. It scratched the hull off a kernel of barley and then ate the grain inside.

"What are you doing?" First Parents asked the ant. "Can you tell us about these seeds and grains?"

The ant said, "Do you know of a spring or a pool or a river?"

First Parents said, "No, we do not know of such things. But we do know of a fountain."

The ant answered, "Then you do know Water. Water is there for you to drink. It is there for you to wash yourselves and your clothing. But Water is also there so that you can grow and cook your food. If you cook each of these grains, each in its own way, you will always have good food. Come with me. I want to show you."

The ant led First Parents to her passageway under the earth.

"This is my path. Come with me." The ant led First Parents up through the passageway and out onto the earth. She led them to a river and said, "Here flows much Water. You can use it to drink, and to wash yourselves and your clothing. And this is also the Water that you can use to cook your grains, after you have ground them up."

The ant led First Parents to a pair of stones and said, "We can use these stones to grind kernels into flour."

The ant helped First Man and First Woman grind some grains into flour. Then the ant showed them how to mix the flower with water, how to make a fire, and how to bake flat loaves of bread.

When they had eaten the bread until they were full, First Man said to First Woman, "Come, let us visit the earth." They took grains of wheat and barley and many other seeds. They wandered here and there. Often, they dropped a few kernels of grain or seeds. Rain fell on them and the kernels and seeds grew into plants.

When First Man and First Woman passed by on their return, they saw the plants, heavy with grain or seed pods. They dug into the earth and saw that each plant had grown from one grain or seed.

"In the future, we will eat half of the grain and plant the remaining half. We will wait until after the first rain falls."

This they did, and that is how the grains and seeds of plants were spread wider and wider, until they could be found growing over much of the earth.

RICE, CORN, MILLET, BEANS, AND WHEAT: WHY THE FIVE GRAINS DIFFER
Hmong Tale

Beans and buckwheat are not grains, but legumes. However, the Hmong apparently believed all of these edible seeds originally came from one type of rice, and therefore put them all in the same grain category.

In the ancient times, all grains were alike. The seeds looked like rice. Yet some grains did not taste like rice, but had the flavor of wheat or corn, millet, or beans. And all of them grew in plenty so that people always had enough to eat.

But in time, the people grew lazy. They did not want to work for their food. The great god Ntzi looked down from above and saw few people in the fields.

"I must find out why they are not working," he said. "I will send my Do Jin out to travel through the countryside so that he can listen to the people.''

The Do Jin was a special person. Even though he always remained in a sitting position, he could move very quickly. The Do Jin sped through the country, stopping to listen wherever he saw a group of people.

''I want to sing and tell stories with my friends. I do not want to break my back planting seedlings,'' he heard one woman say.

Some weeks later, the Do Jin passed a group of children.

''What does it matter if the weeds come and choke a few plants,'' cried one of the children. ''There will always be plenty of grain. We want to play instead of pulling weeds.'' And the children ran off to finish their game of ''snake protecting her eggs.''

When the time of the harvest drew near, the Do Jin approached a group of men standing at the edge of a field of ripe grain.

''Let's sit here under this shady tree and drink beer,'' said one of the men. ''The harvesting can wait.''

The Do Jin hurried back to Ntzi.

''The people are very lazy,'' he reported. ''They do not wish to work.''

Ntzi ordered the Do Jin to return to earth and tear up any plants that were bearing grain.

The Do Jin went back to earth. First he went to the rice fields. As he was about to pull up the stalks, he heard a wailing cry. It came from a woman who had just given birth to her first child.

She pleaded with the Do Jin not to take all the rice.

''If I cannot eat rice I will not have milk to feed my child.''

The Do Jin took pity on her. He gathered up the remaining rice and gave it to her. The woman could feed herself and there would still be enough left to plant the next year.

Next the Do Jin attacked the corn. He pulled it all out except for one stubborn clump. He pulled and pulled until he had stretched the leaves and stalks to three times their usual size. Still he could not get the clump out of the ground. He grasped the tall stalks in the middle and they broke.

Leaving the broken corn stalks, the Do Jin went to search for other plants. When he arrived at the millet field, he slid his hands from the bottom of the stalks to the top. The leaves were dry and sharp, like the edges of knives. They cut the Do Jin's hands and drops of blood fell on the millet fronds, staining them red.

Next the Do Jin went to pull up the bean stalks. Again, the dry husks stung his hands. So he did not twist them off the stalks but left them hanging all over the dry plants.

Now there were only some stalks of regular wheat, and next to it, a few fronds of buckwheat. The Do Jin took pity on the people.

"Wheat is the little sister," he said. "I shall allow these few plants to give seed and come again, but only once, in spring. Buckwheat is the older brother. He must work harder, and come back twice a year."

And the Do Jin gave buckwheat its unique shape of three sides, to distinguish it from wheat.

The following year the people had to work very hard in order to get enough to eat, for there were only a few seeds left from each plant. And each type of seed grew differently.

Of rice, there was the most, because the Do Jin had taken pity on the mother and child. Even today, rice is the most plentiful. It looks the same as always, for it is the first of all grains.

The corn came up in tall stalks with tall, thin leaves, and bore cobs in the middle, just where the Do Jin had broken off the plant.

The millet was rusty red in color, like the drops of the Do Jin's blood.

The bean plants came up bearing pods all over the plant, wherever the Do Jin had crushed the husks.

Little sister wheat had strength to come only once a year, and her grains were smaller than rice. Big brother buckwheat came twice: in late spring and again in autumn, in time to celebrate the New Year.

To this very day, so the Hmong people say, the plants and seeds are much the same as they were after Ntzi sent his messenger, the Do Jin, to teach the ancient humans a lesson. Each seed must be sown, weeded, and harvested in a special way, in order to give a good yield.

Musical Instruments to Make

MAKING SPONTANEOUS NATURAL MUSICAL INSTRUMENTS

Whistles, Tooters, and Squeakers

Place a blade of grass between your hands at the place where they meet when you press them together with the thumbs side by side. Cup the rest of the fingers below, to create a sounding box. Blow until you get a sharp, reedy sound.

Fold a small piece of birch "paper" as shown in the figure. Remember to take this from a fallen tree, not from a live standing one. Cut out a V-shaped hole. Blow as indicated and you will hear a soft whistle.

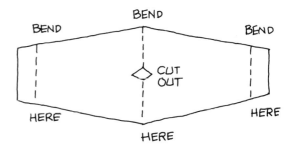

Cut or tear off the stems of plants that have an inner and outer part, such as certain rushes or reeds. Pull out the inner part of the stem, and push back on it. You will get soft, squeaky sounds. Try this with stems of different lengths and varied thickness. Each will produce a different note.

Find an iris, day lily, or any soft, grassy plant that has leaves wrapped in layers around each other. Cut off a piece near the top. Throw away the outer leaves. Open the inner leaves carefully and take out the core leaves. Discard them as well.

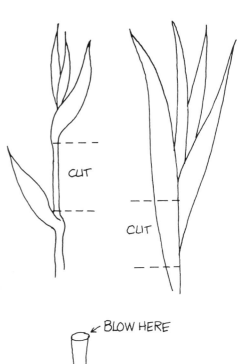

Gently press the remaining leaves back to their original positions. Put your finger on a spot about one inch from the bottom. Blow hard into the opening at the top. With practice, you can get a high, piercing whistle of one or more notes.

Cut off some of the prickly leaf stalks (not the vine) of a pumpkin plant. By sliding the outer layer over the inner you can get a trombonelike sound.

Rattles

Take a branch of shepherd's purse *(thlaspi bursa pastoris)* that has seed pods on it. Bend each pedicel so that each seed pod hangs down on the branch. Then shake and turn the branch until you get a rattling sound.

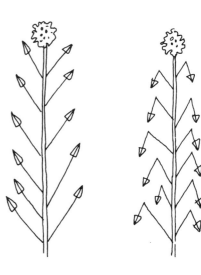

83

Shakers

Try to find an old gourd that has been sitting around for a long time. Often it will dry out inside, leaving the seeds loose. They will make a maracalike sound when the gourd is shaken.

Find large, dried locust tree pods, with the seeds inside. Place a few pods in each hand and shake vigorously.

Drums

Take a length of trunk from a fallen birch tree that is rotting inside. Scrape away the inner part carefully, without cracking or flattening the bark.

Pick two thick, flat leaves large enough to cover the circle at each end of the birch trunk. There should be enough leaf left to lap over on the sides, so that you can tie on the leaves with twined grasses or vines as shown in the illustration.

Play gently on your drum with your fingers or with dried berries on the end of a stem.

Poppers and Snappers

Separate the outer layers of a leaf of the common sedum plant (also called Live Forever). Blow into the cavity until it is pouchlike and full of air. Hold the opening tightly closed and then pop the air out by slapping down hard on the leaf.

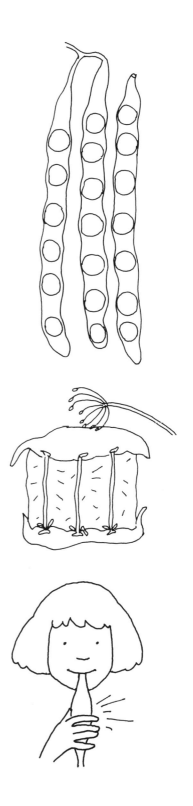

For a series of soft snaps, pop the remaining blossoms on a snapdragon plant that is starting to fade.

Scratchers and Swishers

Rub two pine cones against each other.

Rub two dried cobs of corn against each other.

Swish a leafy branch against a smooth surface and then against a rough one.

Kazoos

Use blades of grass or thin leaves placed between your hands, as for a grass whistle (see above). Instead of blowing, hum and let the leaf vibrate.

Rhythm Band

For a rhythm activity when there are a group of persons who would like to use natural instruments, try doing something like the following, using a strong beat.

Scratch, Scratch	*Swish, Swish*	*Shake, Shake*	*Pop!*
One or more players rub pine cones against each other for two beats.	One or more players swish branches against smooth surface for two beats	One or more players shake locust pods for two beats	One player pops one leaf
Hum, Hum	*Slap, Slap*	*Squeak, Squeak*	
One or more players hum on leaf kazoo for two beats	One or more players slap large leaf against smooth surface for two beats	One or more players play on pumpkin vine trombones for two beats	

Make up your own rhythm band sounds and movements.

Sources of the Stories, Folklore, and Crafts

There is much disagreement about the terms myth, legend, folklore, and folktale. For the most part, I have used the designations as they were given for each story in the sources listed below. If a story was called a myth in one source and a legend or tale in another (or vice versa), I selected the designation given in the earliest source.

"Why Some Reeds Are Hollow" is based on a version told orally to me by Somboon Singkamanen of Thailand.

"Bergamot" is adapted from the story of the same name found in *Seven Peas in the Pod* by Margery Bailey, Boston: Little Brown, 1919.

"The Creation of Plants" is from *Legends of the Jews*, vol. 1, collected by Louis Ginzberg, Philadelphia: Jewish Publication Society, 1909.

"Why Corn Has Silky White Hair" is adapted from "Death and the Old Man," collected by Harold Courlander and published in *Terrapin's Pot of Sense*, New York: Holt Rinehart, 1957.

"Oil Palm and Raffia Palm" is adapted from two versions collected by Mabel H. Ross and published in *"On Another Day . . ." Tales Told Among the Nkundo of Zaire*, Hamden, Conn.: Archon Books, 1979. I also consulted similar stories in Calame-Griaule (see below).

"The Tree and the Ugly Child" is based on a tale collected by G. Clamens, published in *Notes Africaines*, no. 47 (1950). A few elements come from a similar story collected by C. A. Okafor in *The Banished Child: A Study in Tonga Oral Literature*, London: Folklore Society, 1983.

"Rice, Corn, Millet, Beans and Wheat: Why the Five Grains Differ" is adapted from a tale collected by David Crockett Graham and published in *Songs and Stories of the Ch'uan Miao*. Washington: Smithsonian Institution, 1954 (Miscellaneous Collections 123). These people are called Miao by the Chinese but call themselves Hmong.

"Shawondasee and the Golden Girl" is adapted from the version in vol. 2 of Henry Rowe Schoolcraft's *Algic Researches . . . ,* New York, Harper, 1839.

"The Legend of Mondamin" is an amalgam of the version in vol. 1 of Schoolcraft's *Algic Researches* and the one reported by W. M. Beauchamp in "Indian Corn Stories and Legends," *Journal of American Folk-lore,* 11 (1898), 197.

"The Gifts to the Five Nations" is adapted from "Hi-a-wat-ha" by W. M. Beauchamp, *Journal of American Folk-lore,* 4 (1891), 295-306.

"Why Plants Have Human Characteristics" is based on elements pulled from the following sources: Jeremiah Curtin and J. N. B. Hewitt, "Seneca Fiction, Legends and Myths," Bureau of American Ethnology (BAE), *Annual Report 1910-1911,* Washington: U.S. Government Printing Office, 1918; J. N. B. Hewitt, "Iroquoian Cosmology," BAE, *Annual Report 1899-1900,* Washington: U.S. Government Printing Office, 1903; J. W. Powell, "Sketch of the Mythology of the North American Indians," BAE, *Annual Report 1879-1880,* Washington: U.S. Government Printing Office, 1881; Erminnie A. Smith, "Myths of the Iroquois," BAE, *Annual Report 1880-81,* Washington: U.S. Government Printing Office, 1883.

"First Fruits of the Field" is my own translation from Leo Frobenius, *Volksmärchen der Kabylen,* vol. 1 of *Atlantis: Volksmärchen und Volksdichtung Afrikas,* Jena: Eugen Diederichs Verlag, 1921.

Each of the other stories, riddles, and bits of folklore were found in two or more versions in the following books. My versions usually combine elements from several sources. I am especially indebted to the books by Dähnhardt, Dierbach, Folkard, Gubernatis, and Rolland, as well as the multi-volume work *Mythology of All Races,* with its helpful index volume. For those who have access to these works, there is a wealth of plant mythology, legend, and folklore.

   The craft and play ideas with plants were inspired by descriptions in some of these books or by customs passed down in our family. I have included only those that were actually tried out among my family and friends.

Bergen, Fanny. *Animal and Plant Lore.* Boston: Houghton Mifflin, 1899 (American Folk-lore Society, Memoirs, 7).

Blondel, S. *Recherches sur les Couronnes de Fleurs.* Paris: E. Leroux, 1876.

Blumml, E. K. and A. J. Rott. "Die Verwendung der Pflanzen durch die Kinder." *Zeitschrift für Volkskunde in Deutschböhmen und Nieder-österreich*, Berlin, Vol. 11, 1901, pp. 49-94.

Calame-Griaule, Geneviève. *Le Thème de l'Arbre dans les Contes Africains.* 3 vols. Liège: University of Liège, Centre National de Recherche Scientifique, 1969-1974.

Church, Arthur Harry. *The Types of Floral Mechanism.* Oxford: Clarendon Press, 1908.

Cock, Alfons de, and Isidoor Teirlinck. "Kind en Natuur." *Kinderspel und Kinderlust in Zuidnederland.* vol. 6. Ghent: A Siffer, 1906.

Dähnhardt, Oskar. *Natursagen.* Leipzig and Berlin: B. G. Teubner, 1907.

Dierbach, Johann Heinrich. *Flora Mythologica oder Pflanzkunde in Bezug auf Mythologie und Symbolik der Griechen und Römer.* Wiesbaden, 1833.

Eberhard, Wolfram. *Typen chinesischer Volksmärchen.* Helsinki: Suomalainen Tiedeakatemia, 1937 (Folklore Fellows Communications 120).

Folkard, Richard. *Plant Lore, Legends and Lyrics.* London: S. Low, Marston, Searle and Rivington, 1884.

Friend, Hilderic. *Flowers and Flower Lore.* Troy, N.Y.: Nims and Knight, 1889.

Genlis, Madame de. *Jeux Champêtres des Enfants.* Paris: Chez A. Marc, 1822.

Grohmann, Josef Virgil. *Sagen-buch von Böhmen und Mähren.* Prague: Friedrich Beche, 1863.

Gubernatis, Angelo de. *La Mythologie des Plantes.* 2 vols. Paris: C. Reinwald, 1878-82.

Hartland, Edwin S. *English Fairy and Other Folk Tales.* London: Walter Scott, 1890.

Hedleston-Crane, Florence. *Flowers and Folk-lore from Far Korea.* Tokyo: Sanseido, 1931.

Heyden, Doris. *Mitologia y Simbolismo de la Flor en el México Prehispanico.* Mexico: Universidad Nacional, 1983.

Keightley, Thomas. *The Fairy Mythology*. rev. ed. London, George Bell, 1892.

Leske, Marie. *Illustriertes Spielbuch für Mädchen*. Leipzig: Otto Spamer, 1871.

Mythology of All Races. 13 vols. Boston: Marshall Jones, 1916-32.

''On Plants.'' *Pundarika or Lotus of the True Law*. Sacred Books of the East, vol. 21. Oxford, Clarendon Press, 1884.

Porteus, Alexander. *Forest Folklore, Mythology and Romance*. London: Allen and Unwin, 1928.

Rolland, Eugene. *Flore Populaire; ou Histoire Naturelle des Plantes dans leurs Rapports avec la Linguistique et le Folklore*. 12 vols. Paris: Maisonneuve et Larose, 1967; reprint of edition originally published 1896-1912.

Skinner, Charles M. *Myths and Legends of Flowers, Trees, Fruits and Plants*. Philadelphia: J. B. Lippincott, 1911.

Teirlinck, J. *Plantencultus*. Antwerp, Bouchery, 1904.

Wünsche, August. *Die Pflanzenfabel in der Weltliteratur*. Leipzig: Akademischer Verlag, 1905.

Sources of Other Stories
Related to Plants

Flowers

Crowell, Robert L. *The Lore and Legends of Flowers*. New York: Thomas Y. Crowell, 1982. Folklore related to ten common flowers.

An intriguing flower story, based on an old Chinese folk tale, is "Paper Flower." It involves paper cutting and folding. It can be found in *Joining In: An Anthology of Audience Participation Stories and How to Tell Them*. Cambridge, Mass.: Yellow Moon Press, 1988.

Rabinowitz, Louis I. *Torah and Flora*. New York: Sanhedren Press, 1977.

Trees

Kerven, Rosalind. *The Tree in the Moon and Other Legends of Plants and Trees*. Cambridge, England: Cambridge University Press, 1988.

A handkerchief riddle story involving trees planted on the birth of children is "The Peasant and His Plot" in my book *The Family Storytelling Handbook*. New York: Macmillan, 1987.

For an unusual Zulu variant of "The Sacred Story of the Tree of Life," see *Indaba* by Credo Vusamazulu Mutwa. Johannesburg: Blue Crane Books, n.d.

Vegetables

McDonald, Lucile. *Garden Sass: The Story of Vegetables*. Camden, N.J.: Thomas Nelson, 1971.

Those searching for a different pumpkin story for Halloween or Thanksgiving will find it in "An Extraordinary Pumpkin," in the book *Akamba Stories* by John S. Mbiti. Oxford: Clarendon Press, 1966.

Some individual flowers or trees are used as central motifs in stories. They can be traced by using *The Storyteller's Sourcebook* by Margaret Read MacDonald and the indexes to fairy tales and folk tales compiled by Eastman and Ireland, available in most public libraries.

Holidays and Other Special Times to Celebrate Plants

While the stories and activities in this book are meant mostly for spontaneous use, there are times when it is especially appropriate to plan activities centered around plants. Listed below are a few of them. Others can be found by consulting *Chase's Calendar of Annual Events* and the UNICEF Wall Calendar.

Arbor Day. Celebrated in February, April, December, and other times in North America and around the world, depending on when the usual tree-planting season occurs.

Tu B'Shevat. The Jewish New Year of the Trees, held on the fifteenth day of Shevat in the Jewish calendar (generally in February).

Buddha's Birthday. This important feast falls at different times and in different months, depending on the country and the particular form of Buddhism. However, it is always accompanied by flower traditions. See the UNICEF Wall Calendar for correct date each year.

May Day. The first day of May is celebrated in many parts of the world and is often linked with flowers, tree branches, a Maypole, and other celebrations with plants. In Catholic countries and areas, many people still honor Mary, the mother of Jesus, for the entire month, by placing flowers in front of her statue or likeness.

Midsummer Eve or Midsummer Day. In June, this holiday has a wide variety of festive events affiliated with it, particularly in the Nordic countries. Flowers, tree branches, and other plant parts play a distinct role.

Johnny Appleseed Day. John Chapman was born September 26, 1774. Because he devoted his life to spreading apple trees over the eastern and central parts of North America, he came to be known as Johnny Appleseed. Many of the towns and cities where he planted such trees have special events on this day.